PRAYING THE BIBLE: THE PATHWAY TO SPIRITUALITY

Wesley and Stacey Campbell are a dynamic couple and have written a dynamic book. This book is truly revolutionary and offers practical ways to help you grow in your prayer life.

CHÉ AHN
SENIOR PASTOR, HARVEST ROCK CHURCH
PASADENA, CALIFORNIA

In this provocative and challenging book, Wesley and Stacey Campbell provide a valuable resource for those Christians who desire to be obedient to God's command to pray without ceasing but do not know how.

DR. BILL BRIGHT
FOUNDER AND CHAIRMAN, CAMPUS CRUSADE FOR CHRIST
ORLANDO, FLORIDA

Praying the Bible: The Pathway to Spirituality is a rich treasure chest of truth. If your prayer life has grown dull, this book will open up a pathway to God that will change your life.

CINDY JACOBS
COFOUNDER, GENERALS OF INTERCESSION
COLORADO SPRINGS, COLORADO

Wesley and Stacey are truly Elijahs in our day. Their zeal and hunger for prayer are clearly seen in every aspect of their lives. They are eagles of prayer. As people around the world search for that great pathway to His presence, this book is right on time.

BART PIERCE
SENIOR PASTOR, ROCK CITY CHURCH
BALTIMORE, MARYLAND

Having walked down the pathway of Christianity with Wesley and Stacey for several years, I highly recommend that you glean wisdom from their insights to enhance and challenge your own journey with Christ.

DAVID RUIS
PASTOR AND WORSHIP LEADER
WINNIPEG, MANITOBA, CANADA

Information and revelation, empowered by purity and passion, best describe *Praying the Bible: The Pathway to Spirituality*.

DUTCH SHEETS
PASTOR AND AUTHOR
COLORADO SPRINGS, COLORADO

Do you want to accelerate your journey toward the heart of God? If so, here is your road map!

C. PETER WAGNER
CHANCELLOR, WAGNER LEADERSHIP INSTITUTE
COLORADO SPRINGS, COLORADO

PRAYING THE BIBLE

The *Pathway* to Spirituality

WESLEY & STACEY CAMPBELL

Chosen

a division of Baker Publishing Group
Minneapolis, Minnesota

© 2003 by Wesley and Stacey Campbell

Published by Chosen Books
11400 Hampshire Avenue South
Bloomington, Minnesota 55438
www.chosenbooks.com

Chosen Books is a division of
Baker Publishing Group, Grand Rapids, Michigan

Chosen Books edition published 2014
ISBN 978-0-8007-9641-9

Previously published by Regal Books

Printed in the United States of America

The Library of Congress has cataloged the original edition as follows:
Campbell, Wesley.
    Praying the Bible—the pathway to spirituality / Wesley and Stacey
Campbell.
        p. cm.
    Includes bibliographical references and indexes.
    ISBN 0-8307-3126-1
    1. Bible—Prayers. I. Campbell, Stacey. II. Title.
BS680.P64C372 2003
242'.5—dc21   2003000223

Cover and interior design by Robert Williams
Edited by Amy Spence

DEDICATION

To

Caleb, Judah, Joab, Simeon

and Vashti,

We wrote this with you in mind.

May you find, through prayer,

the pathway to God.

You are the motivation behind

most of what we do.

We love you,

Mom and Dad

CONTENTS

FOREWORD

Both from God to Moses and from Jesus to us, we know that the greatest commandment is that we love the Lord our God with all of our heart, soul, strength and mind. This will surely happen! My prayer and passion is to see the first commandment restored to first place. That is why I rejoice to read *Praying the Bible: The Pathway to Spirituality.* Having devoted much time to both praying and leading prayer gatherings, I am convinced that the primary way to grow in love for God, as well as to see His purposes released on Earth, is through *prayer* that flows from understanding God's heart. However, in order to sustain this mighty end-time prayer movement, two things must happen.

First, our hearts must become fascinated with God and prayer must be enjoyable. It's hard to come to God when we feel that He is sad or mad at us. However, when we discover that He really is the glad God in His own holiness and madly in love with us (instead of mad at us), our hearts will open to Him. We need to know that He wants to see us so that we want to see Him. Then as we gaze at His loveliness—like the angels—we will become absolutely fascinated. Our hearts will burn and the fire will fill us with a desire to pray. From there, it is a short step to enjoyable prayer. Isaiah prophesied that in the last day, God would give us joy in the house of prayer:

> And foreigners who bind themselves to the LORD to serve him, to love the name of the LORD, and to worship him . . . these I will bring to my holy mountain and *give*

them joy in my house of prayer. . . . for my house will be called a house of prayer for all nations (Isa. 56:6-7, emphasis added).

Second, joy in the prayer room or enjoyable prayer is what we are seeking to experience in these historic times. Enjoyable prayer will intoxicate our hearts with Jesus. Around the throne, the whole symphony of heaven is worshiping exuberantly with harps and bowls full of incense, which are the prayers of the saints. It is our enjoyable prayer on Earth that is filling the bowls in heaven. With the harp we sing and play God's music, and with the bowls we pray God's prayers. The fascinated heart is key to deep spirituality. Praying the Bible is an excellent resource. That is why I am so enthusiastic about Wesley and Stacey's new book.

Praying the Bible: The Pathway to Spirituality provides a clear "on-ramp" to the practice of enjoyable prayer. This book is so basic and yet so profound in its practical directives of how and why to pray. Few volumes put together the structure of prayer, including the content of prayer (Bible prayers), the times of prayer (daily), the focus of prayer (God), as well as the how-tos of prayer (both out loud and silent). Many books touch on one aspect or another, but it is rare to see them dealt with all together. I rejoice because this book is not full of phrases like "you ought to," "you should" or "why didn't you" without telling you *how* and then giving you the tools to do it. While *Praying the Bible: The Pathway to Spirituality* is very biblical and historical, it is also intensely practical. You will learn things you probably never knew before about how people throughout history, including Joshua, David, Paul and even Jesus Himself, prayed the Bible. Best of all, however, you will learn from this book how to do it yourself, even if you have never prayed the Bible before.

I believe the end-time harvest will not come in the context of fiery intercession. The man leading the intercessory movement is our great high priest, Jesus Christ Himself. That is why we in the Kansas City IHOP are committed to raising up tens of thousands of intercessory prayer missionaries who pray and sing the Bible with fascinated hearts 24 hours a day, 365 days a year. Trained and committed prayer missionaries fill 84 two-hour blocks of prayer each week, complete with prayer leaders, worship teams, sound crews and intercessors. And the main staple of every 24-hour house of prayer is praying and singing the Bible.

Praying the Bible: The Pathway to Spirituality is the book I recommend. Every pastor, prayer leader and intercessor needs this book. It will motivate, inspire and deepen your prayer life, and it will set you on the *pathway to spirituality*.

Mike Bickle
International House of Prayer of Kansas City
www.fotb.com

PREFACE

As humanity neared the end of the second millennium, an amazing grassroots movement began to take place. People everywhere began to pray more than ever before. At first it seemed inconsequential, but then it gathered momentum like a great tsunami. At the end of the age, the scrolls will be opened, and the elders with the living creatures will fall down before the Lamb to worship Him. Each one will be holding harps and golden bowls filled with incense. This incense is called "the prayers of the saints" (Rev. 5:8).

The convergence at the end of the age is clear—full bowls coincide with the release of the scrolls. The scrolls—though releasing judgment—also will bring about the global end-time harvest (see Rev. 7:9-14).

Today it's not uncommon for rank-and-file Christians to engage in 40-day fasts on water and juice for revival. Monthly prayer meetings of up to 500,000 people and annual Holy Spirit festivals of 2 to 4 million people are currently happening in Nigeria. The earth is being united by prayer networks pulling intercessors together from every town, region and country. Worldwide prayer centers, global research and data centers and international strategies make it possible for believers everywhere to click on the Internet and find up-to-date material for any prayer initiative.

With all the modern technologies and the momentum of the Holy Spirit driving the prayer movement, a book like *Praying the Bible: The Pathway to Spirituality* is all the more needed. While prayer is becoming more and more important to everybody—and is spiritually no longer considered the quest of just a few—a book on how to pray and how prayer assists us in our noble pursuit is the answer to the question of the day. For our part, we believe that praying the Bible is the single most important discipline that we can do to cultivate a burning love for God. This is the pathway to attaining a deeper spiritual life.

In brief, *Praying the Bible: The Pathway to Spirituality* is laid out to take you in a progression from here to there. The introduction describes the pursuit of spirituality and the way people have achieved it. We have provided biblical examples of some of the most spiritual men and women of history. Their testimony is all the same—spirituality is achieved through prayer. The introduction challenges us to become like them.

Chapter 1 is about learning to pray. The first step in attaining spirituality is to come to the realization that we must all learn to pray. In the immortal words of the disciples, "Lord, teach us to pray!" the emphasis of chapter 1 demonstrates that everyone has to learn the art of prayer and also shows how we came to that realization.

Chapter 2 stresses the oft-overlooked point that learning to pray is going to be hard work. We must all work at prayer. Many of the most zealous prayer warriors throughout history approached prayer and the pathway to spirituality like athletes in a great contest for the life of the Spirit. Jesus Himself devoted great discipline and hard work to His own practice of prayer. He is our true example.

Chapter 3 proves the point that God calls men and women everywhere to pray every day. Tracing daily prayer from the first commands given to Moses through the life of David and the prophets, we examine the biblical case for daily prayer. Unquestionably, the New Testament Church practiced daily prayer, which went on to shape the attitude of the Church fathers and monastic traditions. This chapter speaks practically to how daily prayer actually has a way of discipling us onto the pathway toward a more spiritual life. It also discusses what will happen if we do not make daily prayer a habit.

Chapter 4 is entitled "Pray to God." The issue here is, To whom are we praying? Contrary to New Age mishmash, The Great Spirit, Yahweh, Allah, Goddess Kali, Shiva, Buddha and the Cosmic Christ are not just different expressions of the same essence. All roads, spiritually speaking, do not lead to Rome. Rather, Christian prayer is praying to God as He says He is, not who we think He is. Therefore, every believer is encouraged to pray the many "visions of God," the theophanies, as revealed to the prophets who saw God with their eyes. From the perspective of the almighty God, seated confidently in His heavenly throne room, our prayers will take on a whole new confidence if we base them on how powerful God is instead of how big our problems are.

Chapter 5 discusses the content of prayer. Having determined to pray to God daily, what does one say? God told Joshua to teach the people to meditate on the Book of the Law. It is our thesis that the people of the Bible prayed the Bible. In other words, God's antidote to those who complain that they don't know what to say is to pray the Bible. This chapter explores the eight distinct prayer genres—Theophanies, the Psalms, Prayers of Wisdom, the Song of Songs, Prayers of the Prophets, the Prayers of Jesus, Apostolic Prayers and Hymns of the Revelation—and why you should pray them. It shows how the great spiritual leaders of the past prayed the Bible and discusses the distinct benefits of praying Bible prayers.

Chapter 6, "Praying Out Loud," provides the answer to the wandering mind. God never intended the novice to struggle to gain focus while praying silently in the head. The command to meditate on the Law was really a call to pray the precepts of the Law out loud back to God. In this chapter, we describe the nature of biblical meditation and how actually to pray the Bible out loud.

Chapter 7 deals with the subject of silent contemplation and how it is very close to the actual attainment of spirituality. Accepting that the goal of our prayer is ultimately the presence of God, silent contemplation takes us from the practice to the presence. This chapter explains the process of contemplation and how our goal of union with God is achieved through it.

The conclusion is a closing challenge for everyone to determine that they will practice the most effective form of personal discipleship—praying the Bible out loud to God every day. We also call on people everywhere to join Jesus in making disciples of all nations. In other words, everyone in this vast world needs to learn to obey or do what God commands—especially the first commandment to love God and pray to Him daily. Let's labor together to see a billion people praying the Bible out loud to God every day!

It also should be noted that we have written and produced this book together. Therefore, in the few times when the word "I" is used, or an illustration is given from the perspective of one and not the other, this should be set in context of the whole. That is, the whole was worked on by both of us, even though a few of the experiences are recorded as singular. Specifically, the

"I" of chapter 6 is Wesley, and the personal experience of chapter 7 is Stacey.

Our prayer is that this one great idea—praying the Bible out loud to God every day—will change your life. We also pray that this great discipline will sweep the earth, fueling love for God and passion for His Son. May His house truly become a house of prayer for all nations.

Bless you in your pursuit,
Wesley and Stacey Campbell

INTRODUCTION

The pursuit of spirituality is universal. No matter where you go on Earth, men and women are incurably religious. Every religion has its own distinctive way of moving people's consciousness from the mundane to the sublime and eternal. To an outsider, these attempts at spirituality might seem bizarre and even ridiculous—like priests wearing funny-looking clothes, following an odd calendar system, abstaining from certain foods (like pork), abstaining from food altogether (as in fasting), going on long and costly pilgrimages, bowing down and praying in public, killing animals in sacrificial rituals and paying a tenth of one's profits to a temple. Yet all of these "bizarre" activities are found and approved of in the Old Testament. However, there are many other ways people attempt to reach a spiritual plateau that are not biblical—Muslims will fast through Ramadan, take long and costly journeys to Mecca and pray five times a day. Hindus will walk naked and unkempt and then wash in the Ganges River to become clean in spirit and body; the Sufis have their whirling dervishes; in Tibetan Buddhist settlements, flapping prayer flags and spinning prayer wheels abound; and New Age proponents arrange crystals on their body to bring about a harmonization of energies. Even people who say they don't believe in God want to attain what they call an authentic or "spiritual" life.

However people do it, the pursuit of spirituality is universal and pervasive on Earth. While many sociologists midcentury were predicting the eclipse of religion in the twenty-first century, the evidence is that there has been a surge of interest in spirituality and in religion. The topic is hot, and we as followers of Jesus Christ need to learn how to exclaim boldly the truth of the Word in an age of rampant untruths.

This book is specifically about Christian spirituality and how to attain it. Although the topic of Christian spirituality is massive, one observation that is pretty much universal is that in order to attain spirituality, one must pray! Throughout history the most radical Christian examples of all time attest to the fact that prayer is the *pathway to spirituality* and that one cannot become a truly spiritual person without it. Saint Catherine of Siena said it this way:

> For perfected souls, every place is to them an oratory, every moment a time for prayer. Their conversation has ascended from earth to heaven—that is to say, they have cut themselves off from every form of earthly affection and sensual self-love and have risen alone into the very height of Heaven.[1]

The goal of spirituality, according to those who have devoted themselves to it, is to live a life in constant communion with God—living in His felt presence. It is the pursuit of one thing, the first commandment—"You shall have no other gods before me" (Exod. 20:3). Spirituality also is the ability imparted from God to live a life that mirrors the image and values of God on Earth as they are in heaven (see Matt. 6:10). In short, a spiritual life is a life transformed by God, manifested in personal holiness and walked out in how we relate to others. This is true spirituality, true religion. Moses touched it; Jesus lived it; Brother Lawrence and the Russian pilgrim testified to attaining it (see chapter 7). Countless others have achieved an awareness of His presence at various times and various levels. However, none who have even remotely touched the realm of God's manifest presence and His power have done so apart from a lifestyle of prayer. Prayer is the single most important ingredient for achieving a state of communion and union with God. Prayer is the *pathway to spirituality.*

PRAYER IS EVERYWHERE

Because the pursuit of spirituality is universal, people everywhere from every culture pray. Newsweek magazine observed that "More people pray than have sex!"[2] People pray for comfort and they pray to get closer to God. Some pray just for help. James, the brother of Jesus, said, "Is any one of you in trouble? He should pray" (Jas. 5:13). People in trouble and those suffering in affliction are told that prayer is the remedy for their troubles. "Is anyone happy? Let him sing songs of praise" (Jas. 5:13). Similarly, the outlet of our joy and thankfulness—our happiness—is also prayer that sings and makes melodies in our heart to God. "Is any one of you sick? He should call the elders of the church to pray over him. . . . And the prayer offered in faith will make the sick person well" (Jas. 5:14-15). Why? Why are we told to do these things? Simply because "the prayer of a righteous man is powerful and effective" (Jas. 5:16). Prayer works! It works not because it is a formula but because God is real and He listens when we talk to Him.

Therefore, if we have determined in our hearts to develop a relationship with God, ultimately we are going to find ourselves drawn toward the place of prayer. There is no way around it. In the Bible, the greatest men and women of the Spirit were men and women of prayer. Scripture says:

> Elijah was a man just like us. He prayed earnestly that it would not rain, and it did not rain on the land for three and a half years. Again he prayed, and the heavens gave rain, and the earth produced its crops (Jas. 5:17).

Think about this: Elijah was a man just like us! And he prayed! When was the last time we put our hand up to heaven and said, "No rain for three and a half years, please," and the heaven stopped its rain; or said "Rain, please," and the heaven gave forth its rain? When was the last time we laid our body on the body of a dead boy—eye to eye, mouth to mouth, hand to hand and body to body—to bring life back to him? When was the last time we called forth life from anything? Elijah did. He communicated with God in a manner that most Christians today know nothing about. Yet, he was a human just like the rest of us. The difference between the supernatural life Elijah lived and the mundane one many of us live is that *he prayed.* The good news is that the same ability to pray to the same God with the potential to yield the same results is within the realm of possibility for any one of us. Elijah was a man just like us—but he prayed.

You will find similar prayer lives behind most of the great patriarchs of the Bible. Noah and Abraham bowed down to God. Isaac said, "Surely the LORD is in this place" (Gen. 28:16), so he set up an altar and called upon God. Jacob prayed to the point of actually wrestling with the angel of the Lord. He was not going to take no for an answer to his prayers (see Gen. 32)! Moses spent days and nights in prayer. The record reads that he made it his custom to go to the tent of the Lord.

> Now Moses used to take a tent and pitch it outside the camp some distance away, calling it the "tent of meeting." Anyone inquiring of the LORD would go to the tent of meeting outside the camp. As Moses went into the tent, the pillar of cloud would come down and stay at the entrance, while the LORD spoke with Moses. The LORD would speak to Moses face to face, as a man speaks with his friend. Then Moses would return to the camp, but his young aide Joshua son of Nun did not leave the tent (Exod. 33:7,9,11).

Notice that Joshua went with Moses to pray and stayed behind after he left. Is there a correlation between this and the fact that it was Joshua, not Caleb, who was chosen to be the next leader of Israel, even though both were men of faith? Was it Joshua's prayer life that propelled him ahead of the rest? Was God looking for a leader who would pursue His presence so that the leader could lead the people to pursue Him in the same way? We cannot overlook the fact that when Joshua was given the mandate of leadership over the children of Israel, his first command from God was not to allow God's Word to depart from his mouth; instead, he was to meditate on the Law day and night (see Josh. 1:8). The mantle of leadership, the promises of God and the command to pray were all given to Joshua simultaneously (see Josh. 1:1-9). Joshua was to lead all of God's people into their inheritance with prayer as their foundation.

JESUS' PRAYER LIFE IS OUR MODEL

If we look further into the lives of significant men of God in the Bible, we will find similar patterns. Samuel prayed, and none of his words dropped to the ground (see 1 Sam. 9:6). David, the shepherd king, cried to the Lord morning, noon and night (see Ps. 55:17). He also remembered the Lord on his bed and meditated on Him through the night watches (see Ps. 63:6). Even through the night, David was praying! If he could have, he would have gazed "upon the beauty of the LORD" all the days of his life (Ps. 27:4). The holy exile, Daniel, following the example of David, prayed three times every day (see Dan. 6:10). It is obvious that the faith these prophets possessed flowed from a solid prayer life. The fruit of their prayers was God touching Earth.

When we move into the New Testament, the testimony of prayer reaches a crescendo in the man Christ Jesus. Surely it must strike us as odd that Jesus, the perfect God-man, seems to pray more than anyone else. When we read through His biography in the Gospels, we see that He is always praying and telling His followers to pray always (see Luke 18:1). In a way, this is confusing. Why did Jesus, the God-man, have to pray so much? If anybody did not have to pray as much during his or her life on Earth, it should have been Jesus. He was the Son of God come in the flesh, yet He prayed and lived out His life as though it really mattered that He prayed!

It is no coincidence that nearly every chapter in the Gospel of Luke shows Jesus praying. Luke writes:

> When all the people were being baptized, Jesus was baptized too. *And as he was praying, heaven was opened* (Luke 3:21, emphasis added).

You might say that this statement encapsulates the ministry of Jesus—"as he was praying, heaven was opened." Immediately after

His baptism, Jesus was compelled by the Spirit to go into the wilderness, where he *fasted* and *prayed* for 40 days (see Mark 1:12-13; Luke 4:1-2). In Luke 5, we read that as crowds came to hear Jesus and be healed of their sicknesses, "Jesus often withdrew to lonely places and prayed" (v. 16). The optimum word here is "often"! Jesus modeled a lifestyle of prayer. He prayed for Himself, and He prayed for others (see Matt. 26:36-39; Luke 22:31-32). He prayed before making critical decisions, such as calling His disciples (see Luke 6:12-13), and He prayed for their continual following (see John 17:6-19). He prayed early in the morning while it was still dark and late at night, all through the night (see Mark 1:35-38; Luke 6:12). Jesus was adamant that Temple life (or synagogue and church) was all about prayer.

> "It is written," he said to them, "'My house will be called a house of prayer,' but you are making it a 'den of robbers'" (Matt. 21:13).

When Jesus prayed, things happened. Luke diligently recorded the dramatic manifestations that occurred when Jesus prayed:

> Jesus . . . went up onto a mountain to pray. As he was praying, the appearance of his face changed, and his clothes became as bright as a flash of lightning (Luke 9:28-29).

When Jesus prayed, doves and voices came down out of heaven, and the dead came to life. Healings, signs and wonders were all part of the dramatic manifestations that occurred when Jesus prayed.

The writer to the Hebrews sums up the prayer life of Jesus:

During the days of Jesus' life on earth, he offered up prayers and petitions with loud cries and tears to the one who could save him from death, and he was heard because of his reverent submission (Heb. 5:7).

Whether it was "very early in the morning" (Mark 1:35), in deserted and "lonely places" (Luke 5:16), all night long (see Luke 6:12) or with an intensity that produced sweat pouring from Jesus' body like "drops of blood falling to the ground" (Luke 22:44), Jesus prayed! He prayed for His disciples, and He prayed for us. Jesus was always praying.

PRAYER IS ESSENTIAL

Why did He do this? Did Jesus know something we don't? Did He understand that everyone's message and authority—even His—came through prayer and connection with the Father in the power of the Spirit? Did Jesus really believe that He could do nothing by Himself (see John 8:28)? And do we really believe that apart from Him, we can do nothing (see John 15:5)? Did He believe that He would receive more words, more power and more authority to do what the Father wanted done if He prayed? If we study His life, we discover that He always knew when it was time to withdraw and pray (see Luke 5:16). Consequently, He never allowed His work on Earth to distract Him from His source of power for the work.

How can it be that today we gloss over this basic truth? Whether it is Moses, Daniel, Elijah, John the Baptist or even

Jesus, the equation is the same—more prayer equals more blessing. There is no question that there is a direct correlation between the people of great prayer and the people with great power. The two cannot be separated. We, too, must come to the realization that if we do not pray, there will not be power. Prayer is not just a good idea, but an actual command! Jesus said, "Men ought always to pray, and not to faint" (Luke 18:1, *KJV*). Paul said, "Pray without ceasing" (1 Thess. 5:17, *KJV*). As one of the greatest Christians that ever lived, Paul said, *"I urge,* then, *first of all,* that requests, prayers, intercession and thanksgiving be made for everyone" (1 Tim. 2:1, emphasis added). So easy to quote, so hard to do.

Under inspiration of the Holy Spirit, Paul *urges* every believer to pray. What he *urges* us is that, "first of all," requests, prayers and intercession be made for everyone. Before even getting to the injunction to pray, Paul qualifies his charge by saying, "first of all." That is to say, I'm urging you before anything else you do—before witnessing, before church attendance, before your job, before your family, before breakfast, if you please—"first of all" to let prayers be made for everyone. Obviously, to this giant of the Christian faith, prayer is a big deal. Paul believed that praying for everyone, saved and unsaved, leaders and followers, changed the world and ultimately affected our own peace and tranquility. Undoubtedly, he learned this from his master, Jesus, who Himself taught that "men [everywhere] ought always to pray, and not to faint [i.e., not stop]" (Luke 18:1, *KJV*).

From the time these commands were given, it is clear that those who heard it understood what it meant. It was common knowledge and common practice that everyone who expected to find God would seek Him every day and every week in prayer.

Whether it was East or West, the desert or the city, what the people of God did was pray. And what was certainly evident is that Christ called His disciples into a relationship with the one true God, in which this relationship manifested and matured through prayer. All that remains today is that we pray.

Jesus said, people "should always pray and not give up" (Luke 18:1). Therefore, the purpose of *The Book of Prayers: The Pathway to Spirituality* is to enable all of us to do just that. And though our spirits are willing and our flesh is weak, nonetheless, Jesus told us to watch and pray so that we don't fall into temptation (see Matt. 26:41). This book is meant to help us fulfill the expectation of all disciples; namely, that we learn to go into our closet alone and pray in secret so that our Father who sees us in secret will reward us openly (see Matt. 6:6). This is what Jesus modeled and taught in the arena of prayer, and when we are fully trained, we will be like our master. We will pray, and in so doing, we will enter the on-ramp of the *pathway to spirituality*, which takes us to the very face of God.

CHAPTER ONE

LEARN TO PRAY

It seems that almost everyone struggles when they begin to learn to pray. Even the greatest of saints testify to a very difficult journey before acquiring mastery in the discipline of prayer. One of these saints was Saint Teresa of Avila who became the first female "Doctor of the Church." Virtually every historian ranks Teresa among the top three personalities in sixteenth-century Spain. Her spirituality shone with unparalleled brilliance.[1] This feisty Spanish Carmelite nun became famous the world over for her tireless work amongst the poor and, especially, for the supernatural, mystical experiences she had when she prayed. So extraordinary were these experiences that her autobiography, *The Life of Teresa of Jesus: The Autobiography of St. Teresa of Avila*, became the standard of what would later be called the Spanish mystics. Her writings helped create the "golden age" (as Spanish historians like to call it) and greatly shaped the subsequent history of the Western Church.[2] Having said that, even this "Doctor" of prayer was repeatedly discouraged because of the difficulty of the discipline of daily prayer.

> Very often I was more occupied with the wish to see the end of my hour for prayer. I used to actually watch the sandglass. And the sadness that I sometimes felt on entering my prayer-chapel was so great that it required all my courage to force myself inside.[3]

At one point, Saint Teresa quit praying altogether for over a year. Even though she had joined the religious life in her teens, she was almost 39 years old before she was able to attain consistency in her prayer life. At that time, she had a vision of the wounded Christ, which propelled her forward in her prayer life. Having overcome, she launched into a prayer life so deep, so full of ecstatic experiences, so rich in the love of God, that she became a leader to all. In her lifetime, she sought to reform the Carmelite order, which had deviated from its original purpose. She founded her first convent in Avila (hence, her name) when she was in her mid-40s and went on to establish 15 additional houses within a 20-year period.[4] This entire time she was sick with a heart condition and suffered two heart attacks. But this did not stop her. To her, the love for God that grew out of one's prayer life was practiced, not merely contemplated.

> Let everyone understand that real love of God does not consist in tear-shedding, nor in that sweetness and tenderness for which we usually long, just because they console us, but in serving God in justice, fortitude of soul and humility.[5]

St. Teresa had things in the right order. She didn't have a works-based relationship with God. True, she did work "to enter that rest" (Heb. 4:11) and labored to learn to pray; however, from that place of prayer, her relationship with God propelled her into works that were exceedingly abundant above her physical capacity. Out of the intimacy of communion with God, all of her works flowed. This is what Jesus modeled to His disciples, and this is the type of example we want to see emulated in the Church today.

We observe two major things from the life of Saint Teresa. One thing is that the art of learning to pray rarely comes naturally. The second thing is that when an effectual, fervent prayer life is attained, it affects the whole of how we live. The reason for this

THE REASON MOST PEOPLE DO NOT PRAY IS NOT BECAUSE THEY ARE FUNDAMENTALLY DISOBEDIENT OR UNSPIRITUAL BUT SIMPLY BECAUSE THEY DON'T KNOW HOW.

book is that we long to teach people to learn to pray. After years of pastoring, our observation is that the reason most people do not pray is not because they are fundamentally disobedient or unspiritual but simply because they don't know how. And when they don't know how, prayer often feels boring, scattered and ineffective. That is why the first step on the *pathway to spirituality* is to determine that you are going to *learn to pray*. If great saints like Teresa of Avila had to learn to pray, so, too, must we learn to pray. For my part, I spent the better part of a decade trying to teach myself how to pray. Stacey learned alone in her room, driven by sheer embarrassment at her lack of Scripture knowledge. Therefore, the seven points in this book—separated into seven chapters—are a distillation of what we have gleaned over our years of learning to pray.

Strangely enough, even the disciples had to learn to pray. They came to Jesus and said, "Teach us to pray, just as John taught his disciples" (Luke 11:1). We say "strangely enough," because the disciples were not novices to the world of prayer. At least one of the disciples (Andrew) was previously a disciple of John the Baptist, and the rest were at least acquainted with his teaching (see John 1:35-40,44). John the Baptist also was a giant of prayer in the world in which they all lived. John the Baptist was likely the most extreme prayer example of that time. Having spent his life set apart from most people, somehow he was able to connect with God more than most. Jesus said of him that there was no one greater born of woman (see Matt. 11:11; Luke 7:28). He was wild and intense, living in the desert on bugs and honey. So enthused was he that people walked out to the desert just to see the "burning man" (see Matt. 3:1-12). John was a wonder of the spiritual world.

Immediately, our curiosity is aroused. What did this man do? How did he become so zealous? The biblical account states that "the child grew and became strong in spirit; and he lived in the desert until he appeared publicly to Israel" (Luke 1:80). It might be said that John chose Mary's needed "one thing" to the utmost (see Luke 10:39-42). When John came of age, he literally marched off into the desert to pray until the word of the Lord came to him. It was there—through many prayers and much fasting—that he received the revelation of how he would recognize the Messiah for whom he was preparing the way (see John 1:33).

THE FORERUNNER OF CHRIST

John the Baptist was the prophesied forerunner of the Messiah (see Isa. 40:3; Matt. 3:3; Mark 1:3; Luke 3:4; John 1:23). John saw himself in this role, and Jesus affirmed it (see Matt. 11:10). As significant as John was as "the voice crying out in the wilderness" just before the coming of Jesus, most believers do not realize how crucial John's desert sojourns were in putting the stamp of monasticism on early Christian spirituality. Toward the end of the third century, Antony of Egypt withdrew from corrupt city life to the desert to clarify his thoughts and draw closer to God. Antony used John the Baptist as his prototype—following John's way of self-mortification through isolation, fasting and wearing uncomfortable clothing. Eventually many others seeking salvation and spirituality joined Antony in the desert. Thus, Antony became one of the first Desert Fathers of the Church and an early founder of Christian monasticism.

Although we do not have much in the way of specific records on John the Baptist's life, some think he may have been familiar with the Essenes, a Jewish sect that practiced asceticism in the desert in Jesus' time. It's important to remember that Judaism at the time of Jesus was not just one uniform religion, but had many variations. The four main branches were:

1. The Sadducees, the rationalist antisupernaturalist skeptics of the day;

2. The Pharisees, the traditionalists who believed in miracles;

3. The Zealots, the ones who wanted to overthrow the Roman military; and

4. The Essenes (not mentioned in the New Testament like the other three), a group that might have evolved out of the *Hasidim* group, the "pious ones," of the Maccabean period (c. 168 B.C.). This group rejected all compromises of Judaism with Greek culture.

The word "Essene" means "healer" in Aramaic, the language of Jesus.[6] Interestingly enough, the Egyptian equivalent of the Essenes was a group called the *Therapeutae,* which also means "the healer" in Greek. Josephus records that there were many Essenes dwelling in every town and that the individuals who belonged to this sect took vows "to first bind [themselves] by solemn exhortations and professions to love and worship God, to do justice towards men, to wrong no creature willingly, nor to do it, though commanded."[7] They rejected the blood sacrifices of the Jerusalem Temple. They practiced voluntary poverty and held all property in common. Their first objective was to keep the first commandment in first place (see Exod. 20:3). What was also unique about the Essenes was that they practiced perennial praise based on the model of Solomon's Temple in the Old Testament (see 1 Chron. 9:33; Ps. 134:1). Their rule states:

> Let the many keep awake in the community a third of all the nights of the year in order to read aloud from the Book and to expound judgment and to sing blessings altogether.[8]

Practically speaking, this meant that during the night, two-thirds of the "Community of Righteousness" (as they were also known) slept in their tents and huts while the other one-third kept up their continual chant of readings, hymns and psalms.[9] John may have known one or more of these Essenes communities that practiced 24/7 prayer and worship.

In time, John left the Essenes and started his own monastic movement in the Judean desert. Gathering disciples, he taught them the disciplines of prayer and fasting. When we read the biblical accounts of John the Baptist, it appears that he was more rigorous in involving his disciples in fasting than was Jesus. The Pharisees once said to Jesus, "John's disciples often fast and pray, and so do the disciples of the Pharisees, but yours go on eating and drinking" (Luke 5:33; see also Matt. 9:14-15; Mark 2:18-20). Jesus explained the reason for this laxity by alluding to the fact that his disciples would have plenty of time for fasting once he was no longer with them.[10] Our point is this: John the Baptist set such a powerful example of prayer that when Jesus' disciples wanted a lesson on prayer, the best example they could find was John the Baptist. They asked Jesus to teach them to pray "just as John taught his disciples" (Luke 11:1).

THE JOURNEY OF A PRAYER WARRIOR

The thought that prayer must be learned is revolutionary to most modern-day Christians. But over the course of our ministry, it is our observation that without a teacher, only the hardiest of souls can excel at this great art of prayer. The rest of us just seem to wander, struggling here and there, feeling very inadequate and inefficient. It is not shameful to admit that we need a teacher, and it is not surprising that it will take time to learn. We want to extend some sympathy to the reader at this point. We understand how hard it is to learn to pray. We ourselves have had many struggles along the way.

MY UNRESPONSIVE TIMES

In fact, like many others, I come from a long line of prayerlessness. Growing up in the Church, there was nothing more boring to me than the prayer meetings. Of course, as soon as I got saved, I was zealous for God, but still the one torture I could not endure was the Wednesday-night prayer meeting. I tried every conceivable way I could think of to get out of having to attend prayer meetings and still be a leader. In retrospect, I must confess that I was saved prayerless, I witnessed prayerless, and I was even a prayerless missionary. I went through four years of Bible college prayerless and even started a church basically prayerless.

Looking back, I don't think I really understood prayer. I didn't know how it worked; I couldn't figure it out. For instance, in the summer we would pray for sunshine for the Sunday School picnic, while at the same time the local Christian farmer whose crops were caught in a drought was praying for rain. What was God to do? Two Christian teams would show up at the same game, each praying, "Oh, God, let the best team win." Of course they both believed that their team was the best team and that God would answer their team's prayer. I also couldn't understand why, when I would pray for people to get better, they would just get worse. The one lady for whom we prayed for healing the most grew worse and finally died. I didn't really believe that God was interested in getting us parking spots. Ultimately, I was confused as to how God could hear the cries of the untold millions living in misery and still want to bother listening to my relatively trivial aches and pains. I just couldn't figure it out. Consequently, I didn't pray.

Eventually I found myself in a theological quagmire. My justification for not praying went something like this: God is all wise and God is all powerful! He knows what's going on, and if it needs fixing, He has the power to fix it. Why then does He want me to go in a room and tell Him what I think is wrong and ask Him to do something about it? He already knows the problem better than I, and undoubtedly, He wants it fixed more than I. The end of this reasoning led me into a semifatalistic faith where I would think loving thoughts toward God but would not really engage in focused prayer. I did what work I was supposed to for God but left the results to Him. In regard to prayer, I was only one step better than a deist.

Coming back to the Bible, I realized that this line of reasoning—taken to its logical conclusion—was really heresy. The Bible says that the effectual and fervent prayers of righteous people do much good (see Jas. 5:16). Even though I knew this, I was unmotivated, because practical help on the subject eluded me. The turning point came through a prophetic encounter. Early in our ministry, while we were in the initial years of planting our church, the Lord moved powerfully in our midst with a great revival. In a single night, He birthed the spirit of prophecy, and many began to "see" in the Spirit.[11] Over a period of three months, at least 70 people, without any prior awareness of such things, suddenly began to shake under the power of the Holy Spirit and prophesy. The first words God gave in prophecy were, "Pray! Pray! Pray! I have called you to be men and women of prayer!" During this awakening, God called us to a life of prayer. Over and over again, He insisted that we pray. Even with this push, I didn't really know how to pray, nor did I feel like the little prayer I did was effective. Though I knew I should pray, I didn't.

Then one night, at a particularly powerful meeting, the spirit of prophecy was again poured out. The awe of God filled the room. People were prophesying here and there. Being the leader, I was the one who wrote the prophecies down as they came. But that night, I began to have this rather distinct feeling that trouble was coming. Sure enough, trouble came. A strong "swoosh" of the presence of God went through the room. Immediately, my wife began to shake and tremble. Suddenly, like Ezekiel being picked up by a lock of his hair, she was propelled like a rag doll across the room and stood up right in front of me. Stacey began to move in front of me with chopping motions of her hands and kicking with short flicks of her feet. Then, like a volcano erupting, she lifted her voice and said, "Wesley . . . Wesley . . . you know what's coming, don't you, Wesley?" Boldly, my wife was standing in front of me, declaring the word of the Lord. God was speaking to me, and yes, I did know what was coming. The prophecy continued: "I have called you . . . and you did not come; I demanded to see you, and you did not show up!" The word went on with a sobriety that brought a hush over the crowd.

Then without warning, another pastor was suddenly hit by the Holy Spirit and jumped to his feet, rushing across the room, bellowing, "Wesley, if you do not pray, your ministry will be taken from you like this piece of paper from your hand, and crumpled up and thrown to the ground!" With that declaration, he ripped the paper right off of my lap and, as a prophetic act, threw it on the ground and stomped on it. Being the discerning man that I am, I knew this was a serious rebuke from the Lord. The fear of the Lord began to grip my heart. That night I determined to change my ways and answer the call to pray.

MY TRYING TIMES

Within days, I was ready. I went out and bought an egg timer to time my prayers so that I would stay the full 30 minutes and not cheat. I had my prayer journal, pens and highlighters. Then I went to my room alone and got everything ready—my favorite chair, all the Bible versions and a pot of tea. Everything was just right. Jokingly, I thought that had I been a woman, I would have gotten candles and had a bath! This was it! I was embarking on my new life of prayer. Turning the timer to 30 minutes, I determined to become God's man of prayer and power for the hour.

Eagerly, I stood up and prayed, "Oh, God! Here I am, in obedience to Your word! And, Lord, I thank You. I thank You for saving me. Thank You that I'm going to heaven and not hell. And, God, thank You for Stacey and the children and for my health, oh, God! In fact, I bless You for everything" [awkward silence, nervous shuffling]. In desperation, I finally invoked the generic missionary prayer of all time: "Africa! God, bless Africa!" Anxiously, I looked at the egg timer. Fearful, I saw that there was no movement at all—not even one minute. My cheeks flushed with embarrassment; I remembered those menacing prophecies as they rang in my ears. Like Elijah, I girded myself up for another run.

"Lord, I'm still here, still calling on Your name. I thank You for my salvation, for Stacey, the kids, my health—arms and legs, fingers and toes—oh, my God [long pause]. China! God, bless China." Again, I sought solace from the egg timer. No noticeable change. Pathetically, I looked up toward the ceiling and said out loud, "You cannot like this?" Right or wrong, I had the distinct feeling that I was boring the Almighty. I began to imagine how God delighted in watching little buttercups growing on mountains that no one would ever see, but *this,* this was pathetic. Crushed, I felt I had no integrity at all. I could not go on, but what was I to do?

Shifting gears, I thought to myself, *I know! I will engage in mental prayer.* (Mental prayer is where one tries to think of God and say things in your head to Him.) I began, *ummhumm . . . umhum . . . ummhhhumm.* Suddenly, a butterfly thought flew through my mind, and like a country dog, I was off chasing those thoughts wherever they led me. It's funny how such thoughts often take you from a cold country to a warm beach somewhere. Without realizing it, I was now daydreaming about sand, surf and sun. I don't know how I got there, but when I came to my senses, I was a thousand miles away from where I intended to be in prayer. Finally, frustrated and discouraged, I got up and left my place of prayer. It was beginning to dawn on me just how difficult this was going to be.

In the months that followed, my prayer life was a rather dismal affair of stops and starts with only a slight whiff of anointing now and again—nothing of which it could be said, "This was the Lord's doing, and it is marvellous in our eyes" (Mark 12:11, *KJV*). Then I remembered a piece of sage advice from my father: When you don't know how to do something, find someone who does it better than you and ask them to teach you how to do it. Around that time, I heard about this guy called Mike Bickle, who, legend had it, prayed three to five hours a day. Not only that, he even made his pastoral staff pray three to five hours a day! This was the most outrageous thing I had ever heard. What on Earth would anybody say to God for five hours a day? I wondered if such a prayer life were even possible.

MY SEEKING TIMES

Intrigued, I set out to Kansas City to see this phenomenon for myself. I have to admit that I was surprised at what I found. I found people who really did pray five hours a day. It was amazing. And when I discovered that they actually liked it, I was even more astonished. Going directly to the church bookstore, I said, "Give me everything that man has written on the subject of prayer." "Written?" the clerk incredulously responded, "He hasn't written anything; he just prays all the time." "Then how am I going to learn this?" I asked worriedly. "Well," said the clerk, "he does have a lot of teaching tapes on the subject. Maybe these would help?" I excitedly responded, "Good, give me all you've got!" Like a boy in a candy store, I loaded up my suitcase with more than 100 tapes. I was going to learn this thing called prayer!

It took me over 18 months to get through those tapes and a number of other good books. In the end, I boiled it all down to a few good points. Though I didn't realize it at the time, Mike Bickle's prayer model is actually based on the timeless, historical model of prayer used by men and women of God for over

3,000 years. It was the model that came out of the cradle of Judaism, which was practiced by everyone in the Early Church. Catholic and Orthodox traditions have labeled it the *lectio divina,* the divine reading. In fact, after 10 years of intensive study on the subject of prayer, we have found that the modern-day evangelical/charismatic Western Church may be the first sector of the Church in over 3,000 years to not do prayer right!

> OUR MODERN-DAY EVANGELICAL/ CHARISMATIC WESTERN CHURCH MAY BE THE FIRST SECTOR OF THE CHURCH IN OVER 3,000 YEARS TO NOT DO PRAYER RIGHT!

MY DECISIVE TIMES

Knowing that I needed help to learn to pray was my starting point. Stacey's story is different, yet similar. Today we are convinced that everyone must come to the understanding that they have to learn to pray. If you don't pray as well as you want to right now, take heart, you can learn. If you are a parent, you must begin to teach your own children to pray as soon as they can talk. If your children are already teenagers, it will be more difficult, but you will have to start there. If we are already adults ourselves and have never really learned the art of prayer, we must begin today. We must simply take on the attitude of a disciple and cry out, "Lord, teach us to pray!"

CHAPTER TWO

WORK AT PRAYER

Saint Benedict called prayer *Opus Dei* in Latin, "The Work of God," and devoted 20 percent of his famous Rule to teaching his followers how to put it into practice. Summarizing *The Rule of Benedict,* Stead remarks:

> The "Work of God" consists in the reading (out loud), or chanting, of the Word of God, and a few ecclesiastical compositions based on the Word, like hymns or commentaries.[1]

Like the disciples of Jesus, Saint Benedict realized that prayer was something that had to be learned. Therefore, it is not surprising that as with any discipline, hard work precedes proficiency in this spiritual skill. All good athletes recognize the principle of discipline before delight! The same is true of prayer. Becoming skillful in prayer will take intense focus and *a lot* of hard work. Of course, Western Christianity hardly has a grid for such a concept even though history is replete with it. So it is best that we settle the issue at the outset: Prayer will be hard work, it may be boring and we have to commit to it for the long haul, but there is a guarantee of joy if we persevere (see Heb. 12:1-2).

When we get right down to it, most of us are just plain lazy when it comes to prayer. That is because we have not cultivated a taste for the real thing. For many of us, our favorite prayer posture is either sitting on a chair or lying comfortably in bed, nestled on a fluffy pillow. Sleepily, we think our prayers. (We don't even have the energy to say them out loud!) *Oh, my God, I thank You for this day—and now, as I lay me down to sleep, I thank You, Lord—my soul to keep. And—dear God—zzzZZZ.* When we awake eight hours later, we wonder at the lack of vitality in our prayer life.

Isaiah observed the same phenomenon in his day. He lamented:

No one calls on your name or strives to lay hold of you (Isa. 64:7).

Other versions translate the word "strives" as "stirs" or "arouses himself to take hold of Thee" (Isa. 64:7, *NKJV, NASB*). Paul said of his fellow worker, Epaphras, *"He is always wrestling in prayer for you"* (Col. 4:12, emphasis added). Other descriptive terms used alongside prayer in the Bible would include words like "loud cries and tears" (Heb. 5:7), "travail of his soul" (Isa. 53:11, *KJV*), "effectual" and "fervent" (Jas. 5:16, *KJV*), "night and day" and "fastings" (Luke 2:37; 1 Tim. 5:5, *KJV*) and "more earnestly" (Luke 22:44, *KJV*). These phrases connote anything but passivity! In fact, the aggressive model of prayer found in the New Testament led later disciples of Christ to create a spiritual culture of ascetics known as the spiritual athletes. Such men and women certainly did not play at prayer.

IT TAKES HARD WORK

Saint Antony of the Desert was one such man. Taking his cue from John the Baptist, Antony literally followed the descriptions of the heroes mentioned in Hebrews 11. Like John, Antony "wandered in deserts and mountains, and in caves and holes in the ground" (Heb. 11:38). Although he came from a rich family, Antony gave up his entire inheritance. In place of a life of luxury, Antony went off to practice asceticism, or "the discipline" (as it was originally called). Within Antony's lifetime, this discipline evolved into monasticism. Antony so excelled at this monastic lifestyle that *Christian History* magazine calls Antony, "the best there ever was."[2] At first, Antony gave himself to constant prayer and working with his hands.[3] Then he went on to severe fasts and sleep deprivation. Antony ate only once daily after sunset, but there were times when he only took food every second and frequently even every fourth day. When he did eat his food, it was bread, salt and water. Finally, still unsatisfied with his progress, he moved outside the village and took a tomb for his home. Closed up in the tomb, Antony battled demons that

FOLLOWING SAINT ANTONY'S EXAMPLE, THOUSANDS OF ZEALOUS PRAYER WARRIORS FOLLOWED ANTONY'S PATHWAY INTO THE DESERT, DIGGING CAVES OUT OF ROCKS, BUILDING TOWERS TO ESCAPE CROWDS AND GENERALLY PARTICIPATING IN ALL SORTS OF SUPERHUMAN ANTICS IN ORDER TO CONFIRM THEMSELVES ACCORDING TO THE DISCIPLINE OF ASCETICISM—THE *PATHWAY TO SPIRITUALITY*.

whipped and assailed him with such force that he lay on the earth speechless from the tortures.[4] There in his "heavenly home," Antony prayed, fought with demons and disciplined himself. After 20 years of neither going out nor being seen by anyone, Antony emerged at about 40 years old.

Those who saw him were amazed to see his body unchanged and his soul faultless. Soon many were eager to imitate his asceticism. For the next 65 years, Antony enjoyed mystical experiences, prophecy, miracles and power over demons. Antony lived to the ripe age of 105, and in A.D. 357, the year after his death, Saint Athanasius wrote the famous *Vita Antonii*, or *The Life of St. Antony*. This biography became a runaway best-seller, setting the imaginations of the Early Church on fire. Thousands of zealous prayer warriors followed Antony's pathway into the desert, digging caves out of rocks, building towers to escape crowds and generally participating in all sorts of superhuman antics in order to confirm themselves according to the discipline of asceticism—the *pathway to spirituality*. This, of course, was all patterned after the greatest of Christian heroes, John the Baptist. Philip Schaff, in his *History of the Christian Church,* writes:

> A mania for monasticism possessed Christendom, and seized the people of all classes like an epidemic. . . . Nothing was more common than to see from two to five hundred monks under the same abbot. It has been supposed, that in Egypt the number of anchorites and cenobites equaled the population of the cities.[5]

> [Famous historian] Gibbons adds the sarcastic remark: "Posterity might repeat the saying, which had formerly been applied to sacred animals of the same country, that in Egypt it was less difficult to find a god than a man."[6]

Philip Schaff says of the increase of monks:

> Nothing in the wonderful history of these hermits in Egypt is so incredible as their number.[7]

In spite of the rich testimony we have in the Church, many of us who are just beginning to pray underestimate the work and resolve that is needed to become adept at it. Not only do we rarely teach and practice fasting—let alone mortification in prayer—even basic energy and enthusiasm is discouraged. Discipline and structure is called legalism. Zeal is labeled emotionalism. Yet every leader in the New Testament, including

Jesus, Peter, John and Paul, would have learned to pray by hard work. The accumulated time, habit and depth of prayer that they would have attained by the time they were 18 years old would be greater than that which most adults of today will ever reach in their lifetime. The work that *all* parents in biblical times would have put into training their children to pray would boggle the minds of most modern-day parents. Thus, in our contemporary Western, nonpraying culture, growth in prayer will not happen without resigning ourselves to the fact that we are in for some hard work and serious catch-up.

JESUS WAS RAISED IN TRADITION

A most interesting question is, How did Jesus pray? Did He have a structure? Did He use rote prayers? Did He pray every day? Did He sit, stand, walk or lie down? Can we know what He said? Can we know how Jesus prayed?

Contemporary Christianity tends to overlook the fact that Jesus was a man born in time and space and was the same as all the other men born of women, in the sense that He was a living, breathing human being. Of course, He was unlike all other men because He was God in the flesh, thus He was perfect. In His day, Jesus had trouble convincing people of His divinity and perfect ways (see Matt. 13:54-57; Mark 6:3; Luke 4:22; John 6:29; 7:25-30). However, in our day, we have trouble convincing people of His humanity. Almost no one feels compelled to be like Jesus, because they think, *Well, He was Jesus, the God-man, and how can I be like Him?* But one of the cardinal doctrines of the Church affirms that Jesus was fully God *and* fully man—the glorious "*man* Christ Jesus" (1 Tim. 2:5, emphasis added). As a man, Jesus spoke Aramaic, Hebrew and perhaps some Greek—the vernacular languages of His region. He dressed the way all the other Hebrews dressed. He followed the customs of His time and place, rather than the customs of, say, China or Europe. We have to consider the fact that the man Christ Jesus was born into a particular time, a place, a people, a belief system and a religious structure. What's more, Jesus fulfilled all things—keeping the Law and following the customs of His day (see Deut. 7:11).

For example, Jesus was brought to the Temple on the eighth day because it was time for Him to be circumcised. When the time of purification, according to the Law of Moses, had been completed, Joseph and Mary took Him to Jerusalem to present Him to the Lord (see Luke 2:21-22). Why? Because "(as it is written in the Law of the Lord, 'Every firstborn male is to be consecrated to the Lord)'" (Luke 2:23). It is recorded that "the parents brought in the child Jesus [to the Temple] to do for him what the *custom of the Law required*" (Luke 2:27, emphasis added). Luke goes on to say, "When he [Jesus] was twelve years old, they went up to the [Passover] Feast, according to the *custom*" (Luke 2:42). When Jesus began His ministry, "He went to Nazareth, where he had been brought up, and on the Sabbath day he went into the synagogue, *as was his custom*. And he stood up to read [the Scriptures]" (Luke 4:16, emphasis added). The reason it says "as was His custom" is because Jesus did this every Sabbath. A cursory reading of the New Testament will show that Jesus meticulously followed the time-honored practice of going to synagogue and teaching in synagogues He visited (see Matt. 4:23; 9:35; Luke 4:44; John 18:20). Thus, if it is true that Jesus observed the customs, practices and rituals of the Law, then what about the custom of Jewish prayer?

JESUS' MODEL OF PRAYER WAS JEWISH PRAYER

It's obvious that Christian prayer grew out of the Jewish prayer model. Ignorance about this fact within the Christian Church is startling. For instance, it was credibly reported that a rabbi was giving an address on Jewish worship to a group of Christians visiting his synagogue. Following the talk, one of the visitors was heard to observe, "Well, now, isn't that interesting . . . *they* even use *our* Psalms!"[8] It must always be remembered that it is the Gentile Church that was grafted into the Jewish "olive tree" (Rom. 11:24), not vice versa. Therefore, in order to understand how Jesus and John the Baptist would have taught their disciples to pray, one must first begin by looking at the Law, or Torah. In it, we find an elaborate system of laws and rituals concerning prayer that predates the New Testament Church by at least 1,500 years.

Since the Church grew out of this Jewish context, what would the earliest Church have understood about Jesus' sermons on prayer? Remember that the entire first generation of the Early Church did not have the New Testament Scriptures as we do now, simply because they weren't written yet. In fact, the disciples understood that their faith was essentially a "fulfilled Judaism" which had found its long-awaited Messiah. They definitely continued to use "the Law of Moses, the Prophets and the Psalms" (Luke 24:44) as their Scriptures. The New Testament Epistles, it seems, were almost like commentaries for interpreting the Old Testament in light of the "having come" Messiah. Many of Paul's ethical teachings were Old Testament prophetic applications and exhortations on how we should live. The

Gospels, written much later, were unique *hagiography* (holy biography), supplying the life and testament of Jesus Christ. So the Early Church was made up primarily of Jews who now understood that it was time to fulfill their real calling by becoming a blessing to all peoples (see Gen. 12:1-3) and "a light to the Gentiles, that You should be My salvation to the ends of the earth" (Isa. 49:6, *NKJV*; see also Isa. 9:2; 42:6).

PRAYER AS A WAY OF LIFE

This has definite implications when it comes to the basic practice of prayer, as derived from the Book of the Law. The Messianic Jews would have continued to pray the same way they always had, and the Gentiles (i.e., non-Jews) who came to believe in the Messiah would have adopted the model and style of Jewish prayer with modifications and additions of a new and growing faith. This being the case, what would the practice of prayer in the Early Church have been? Obviously, it would have been Jewish prayer, and Jewish prayer was shaped from the most famous passage in the Pentateuch, the Shema. According to the Babylonian Talmud, Jewish boys were taught this passage as soon as they could speak (*Sukkah 42a*).[9] The Talmud further specifies that the "the father must teach him."[10] It is safe, then, to assume that Joseph would have taught his son, Jesus, how to pray the Shema.

> Hear, O Israel: The LORD our God, the LORD is one. Love the LORD your God with all your heart and with all your soul and with all your strength. These commandments that I give you today are to be upon your hearts. Impress them on your children. Talk about them when you sit at home and when you walk along the road,

when you lie down and when you get up. Tie them as symbols on your hands and bind them on your fore-heads. Write them on the doorframes of your houses and on your gates. . . . then when you eat and are satis-fied, be careful that you do not forget the LORD, who brought you out of Egypt, out of the land of slavery. Fear the LORD your God, serve him only and take your oaths in his name (Deut. 6:4-9,11-13).

The Shema was central to the whole of life. In his classic work, *To Be a Jew,* Rabbi Hayim Halevy Donin writes:

To engage in prayer is the most obvious and the most universal reflection of man's relationship with God. Prayer in its highest form and at its most sincere levels is called a "service of the heart," and constitutes one of the many ways by which love of God is expressed. "And you shall serve the Lord your God" (Exod. 23:25). According to Maimonides, this refers to prayer, for he relates it to "And you shall serve the Lord your God with all your heart." According to the Sages, the latter part of the verse is a reference to prayer (tefilah).[11]

Simply put, the first of the Ten Commandments, to worship the Lord your God (see Exod. 20:1-6; Deut. 5:6-10); the Shema, "Love the LORD your God" (Deut. 6:5); and the oft-repeated com-mandment "to serve the LORD your God" (Deut. 10:12; see also 11:13) are all fulfilled first and foremost in prayer. Prayer was at once the means and proof of our love as well as the impetus to obey and serve the Lord. This tradition of prayer among Jews as a "service of the heart" extends to a period of time long before the Temple was destroyed in A.D. 70.[12]

From the commandments of the Lord, the Jews developed various rituals, which served as reminders for directing worshipers into the presence of God. Some of the symbols used in prayer were the *tefillin*—two small wooden boxes wrapped in leather and filled with parchments of Scripture; the *mezuah*— more small scrolls of Scripture attached to the door frame of every house (see Deut. 6:9); the *tzitzit*—fringes attached to four-cornered garments that reminded the wearer to observe all the commandments (see Num. 15:37-41) and the *tallit*—the prayer shawl, which hosted the fringes during prayer (*Hil. Tzitzit* 3:11). These would all have been part of the customs that Jesus was used to.

Before anyone rolls their eyes and says, "That's so religious," we must remember that it was God Himself who commanded that these rites be observed by His people. A legitimate question is, Why did God want these symbols? Rabbi Saul (later known as the apostle Paul) said that "the law was our tutor to bring us to Christ" (Gal. 3:24, *NKJV*). It appears that in the very doing of the ritual, the Lord was trying to instill something about Himself. Obviously, He did not want these forms to become vain traditions. On the contrary, God wanted them done from the heart with passion.

Take the tallit (prayer shawl) and tefillin (phylacteries). Both are Jewish customs derived indirectly from Scripture. The tefillin are small black leather boxes worn on the wrist and forehead by Orthodox and Conservative Jewish males during morning prayers. They contain small parchment scrolls upon which are written specific biblical passages (see Exod. 13:1-16; Deut. 6:4-9;

11:13-21). In each passage, there is a reference to binding something as a "sign," "token" or "memorial" on the hands and forehead. The Bible doesn't actually say to strap black leather boxes onto your body—the passages might be symbolic or metaphoric. However, the Jewish faith and devotion interpreted them as literal commands.

As a Jew, Jesus would have been taught to pray and recite blessings and prayers as soon as He could speak and every day of His life thereafter. Imagine His joy, then, at the time of His bar mitzvah, when He donned the tefillin for the first time. If you or I were allowed to be a guest at Joseph and Mary's house and could have written down what we observed, what would we have seen? As an imaginative exercise, we might have seen something like this:

> The young Jesus came into the prayer room and began to wash His hands in the prescribed ritualistic manner. Barely 13, His voice cracking with puberty, He stood to recite the first portions of His morning blessing formula. Following the blessings, Jesus reverently looked to heaven and spoke again, "God, make My words pleasant today." After two further blessings, Jesus took a four-cornered type of prayer undershirt and placed it over His head and shoulders, letting it come to rest on His body. This special garment would be worn all day under His other clothes. Then Jesus wrapped Himself within His tallit, or prayer shawl, and recited more blessings.
>
> After this, carefully, and with great meaning, Jesus began the most demonstrative and time-honored act of His morning prayer time: the putting on of the tefillin.

This was the first time He would officially put it on, but from now on, Jesus would don it every day for the rest of His life. He did not divert His eyes, nor engage in conversation, as at this point it was forbidden. Then, just like He had practiced in preparation for this moment, Jesus took the tefillin in His writing hand and bound the small leather box of Scriptures upon the bare bicep of his weaker hand. Now, the Scriptures were occupying the area closest to His heart, thereby fulfilling the command to place these words upon His heart (see Deut. 6:6; 11:18). Next, the son of Joseph paused and began to recite more blessings.

Resuming the task, Jesus tightened the strap of the tefillin, and wound it seven times around His forearm just below the elbow. The remaining strap was held in His palm. Now it was time for the head tefillin. The elaborate process continued as Jesus placed the box above His forehead, but not below His hairline. Carefully, He adjusted the symbol so that the box was on a line between the eyes, for it is written that these words shall be a sign between your eyes (see Deut. 6:8, *KJV*). As Jesus bound these phylacteries upon His body, He prayed the following words: "Blessed art Thou, Lord our God, King of the universe, who has sanctified us with Thy commandments and commanded us concerning the mitzvah of tefillin. Blessed be He whose glorious majesty is forever and ever."

Now that the head tefillin was firmly in place and blessed, Jesus unwrapped the leather ends He had laid across His palm and rewound them three times around

His middle finger, and then rewound the remaining strap around His palm. As He did this, He repeated the beautiful words of the prophet Hosea:

I will betroth you to Me forever; yes, I will betroth you to Me in righteousness and justice, in lovingkindness and mercy; I will betroth you to Me in faithfulness, and you shall know the LORD (Hos. 2:19-20, *NKJV*).

Now that He was fully clothed in the proper manner for addressing His Father in heaven, Jesus kissed the Torah, making sure He was not facing a painting or a mirror, and raised His hands toward the Temple Mount. With feet together, He began praying the standard Eighteen Benedictions. These benedictions were believed to have been instituted by Ezra. Whether or not this is true, everyone knew they were hundreds of years old. Sometimes bending and bowing, sometimes bobbing and swaying, Jesus prayed, cultivating his *kavanah*—intention and direction. His father had strictly taught Him never to let His prayer become merely routine, for that was not even considered supplication. He had even heard of how some pious Jews of old would wait for an hour before reciting their prayers, hoping to develop *kavanah,* or the appropriate state of mind to speak to God. As was customary at the opening of every benediction, Jesus bent His knees at the word "blessed," bowed His head at the words "are You" and straightened out again at the word "Adonai."

The whole while Jesus was doing this, it was clear that He knew there was to be no idle talk or chatter, and no distractions or silly playing. He performed His "service of the heart" in light of the favorite reminder He had seen inscribed on the walls of synagogues—"know before whom you are standing."[13]

After He prayed the Eighteen Benedictions, Jesus stretched out His arms toward the Temple and boldly declared the Shema. This was followed by more readings from the Scriptures. Finally, He began to untie the tefillin as carefully as He had tied it. In all, He must have spent at least 30 minutes engaged in this private "service of the heart."

It must be noted, as well, that at the same time Jesus was performing His prayers, all throughout the holy city, thousands of others were offering up the same prayers and rituals in keeping with the morning and evening Temple sacrifices. From that point on, perhaps three times a day, Jesus began to engage in this holy office. He would recite the Shema. There would also be extra blessings and prayers said upon rising, going to bed, working and eating. On top of all this, there were the Sabbath and the many other special holidays and festivals throughout the year when Jesus would offer special prayers. This day was the first of His official prayer times, but it was really only the beginning of a lifestyle.

PRAYER AS A NECESSITY

Of course, the tendency of all symbolic acts is to forget the intention and glory in the symbol. Jesus Himself rebuked those who "make broad their phylacteries, and enlarge the borders of their garments" (Matt. 23:5, *KJV*), or prayer shawls. Without minimizing the danger for abuse, Jesus did not deny the potential for good. He said the following were good disciplines: "When you give to the needy" (Matt. 6:2); "When you pray, . . . this, then, is how you should pray" (Matt. 6:5-9); and "The time will come when . . . they will fast" (Matt. 9:15). Jesus affirmed these time-honored disciplines when they were done without hypocrisy and practiced in the context of justice, mercy and faithfulness. He maintained that it is possible to "have practiced the latter, without neglecting the former" (Matt. 23:23).

Jesus lived amongst a people who rose (and still do rise!) daily and recited the following creed while they put on their morning and evening tefillin:

I am now intent upon the act of putting on the Tefillin, in fulfillment of the command of my Creator, who hath commanded us to lay the Tefillin, as it is written in the Torah: And thou shalt bind them for a sign upon thine hand, and they shall be for frontlets between thine eyes. Within these Tefillin are placed four sections of the Torah, that declare the absolute unity of God, and remind us of the miracles and wonders which he wrought for us when he brought us forth from Egypt, even he who hath power over the highest and the lowest to deal with them according to his will. He hath commanded us to lay the Tefillin upon the hand as a memorial of his outstretched arm; opposite the heart, to indicate the duty of subjecting the longings and designs of our heart to his service, blessed be he; and upon the head over against the brain, together with all the senses and faculties, is to be subjected to his service, blessed be he. May the effect of the precept thus observed be to extend to me long life with sacred influences and holy thoughts, free from every approach, even in imagination, to sin and iniquity. May the evil inclination not mislead or entice us, but may we be led to serve the Lord as it is in our hearts to do. Amen.[14]

Meir Jung, a distinguished nineteenth-century rabbi, said, "This commandment, performed daily, has contributed more effectively to preserve and to further the morality of our people than have all the learned books on ethics written by our religious philosophers."[15]

Rabbi Jung is right. Imagine if every Christian in every conservative, evangelical and charismatic tradition rose every morning to actually go through the motions of tying verses to their arms and forehead. Imagine if they earnestly recited blessings and prayers, asking to keep their thoughts and actions free from sin and iniquity. Imagine

> THIS COMMANDMENT OF PUTTING ON THE TEFILLIN, PERFORMED DAILY, HAS CONTRIBUTED MORE EFFECTIVELY TO PRESERVE AND TO FURTHER THE MORALITY OF OUR PEOPLE THAN HAVE ALL THE LEARNED BOOKS ON ETHICS WRITTEN BY OUR RELIGIOUS PHILOSOPHERS.

if they recited passages of the Psalms, the Law and hymns daily. Imagine if they prayed (even if by rote) 18 separate prayers and blessings. Imagine if they did this every day. Would this make a difference? We believe that it most certainly would. However, the sad fact is that most modern Christians barely check in mentally with God as they go about their day.

I am not saying that we ought to do specific rituals or copy the complete prayer procedure that God gave at Sinai—or the Jewish customs that developed later. The question of obedience to the Law was settled at the first council of Jerusalem. When the Judaizers wanted to place the yoke of circumcision and the Law of Moses on the necks of the Gentile believers, the apostles said no! James, the brother of Jesus, gave the final word on this:

> It is my judgment, therefore, that we should not make it difficult for the Gentiles who are turning to God. Instead we should write to them, telling them to abstain from food polluted by idols, from sexual immorality, from the meat of strangled animals and from blood (Acts 15:19-20).

It is evident that at this time God initiated a way of coming to Him that was not flippant and casual. The purpose of all these acts, when done with meaning, was meant to move our affections and facilitate love for God. Worship, praise, thanksgiving, petition and intercession—these were all a lot more intense than reciting, "Now I lay me down to sleep. I pray the Lord my soul to keep . . . " Jesus, along with everyone else in His day, worked on His own prayer life. It was not passive, nor was it something that someone could observe and do for Him. Parents prayed for their children but did not pray to replace their children's prayers. Pastors and rabbis did not pray while everyone else sat silent. No, every person had to engage in prayer for *themselves*. And somewhere in the midst of this prayer experience, the individual would feel God. This is the reason why Jesus, John, Paul and all of the disciples and the Early Church worked at prayer.

Therefore, we see that the New Testament Church had a thoroughly Jewish constituency who accepted Jesus of Nazareth as their Messiah and who also continued to worship as they had been taught for hundreds of years. It never occurred to these Jewish believers in Jesus that their beliefs about God and His character and about prayer and morality would undergo any fundamental changes. However, as more and more Gentiles came to believe in Jesus and became "grafted on" to the Jewish "olive tree" (Rom. 11:17,24), Jewish traditions that were particularly Jewish, such as tefillin and tallit, Sabbath keeping, maintaining a kosher house and circumcising, came into question and ultimately became optional. Gentiles who came to believe in Jesus were not compelled to follow these various Jewish traditions, but Jewish believers who wanted to keep their traditions continued to get close to God in the ways in which they had grown up and were familiar.

THE IMPLICATION OF ALL THIS IS HUGE!

Since this was the context of the entire New Testament Church population, most of whom had been trained from childhood onwards in Jewish-style mechanics of prayer, what are the implications for us today? These believers learned structure before they felt inspiration. They knew discipline before delight. They would have had a serious prayer vocabulary before they experienced a "swoosh" of the Spirit. Jesus said of these holy scribes, "Therefore every scribe who has become a disciple of the kingdom of heaven is like a head of a household, who brings forth out of his treasure things new and old" (Matt. 13:52, *NASB*). The New Testament teaching on prayer was pulling from *some things new* and *some things old*. The disciples knew and taught that we must labor in prayer.

WE NEED TO TEACH OUR CHILDREN HOW TO PRAY

One of the implications for today is that we, too, must teach our children to pray. This is not a Christian option! As much as adults need to learn to pray, so children also need to learn. If parents do not teach their own children to pray, the children will pray even less than their parents. It is sad that parents think their children will somehow learn in a vacuum. Experience bears out that children do not learn well by osmosis—unless they are learning to pray as little as their parents do! They must be instructed in how to pray. It is our God-given duty to teach our children to be friends of God. Unless we, ourselves, learn how and then teach our children how, they will not learn. Consequently, they will not pray. The entire process will take work.

WE NEED TO TEACH OURSELVES HOW TO PRAY

The second application is that Jesus and the Jews of the Bible worked at this thing called prayer. Sure, all of us can conjure up caricatures of Jews at the Wailing Wall, ringlets dangling under their hats, books in hand, bobbing back and forth in their times of prayer. We smirk and discount it as cultural fanaticism. But the fact is that we can learn some important lessons from these people. It's a lesson in intentional behavior. Whether Orthodox Jews feel like it or not, they are not just going through the motions of prayer or daydreaming while praying. They are not drifting off to sleep as they close their day with a pillow prayer. Instead, they are fully engaged—head, heart, body and mind. They are making a decision of the will to engage the Almighty.

> The rabbis understood that fixed prayer was only a starting point. To speed through devotions without feeling, vainly babbling rote prayers was not really praying at all. For prayers to reach heaven the rabbis said, "they need *kavanah*"—literally translated "intention" or "direction." As Rabbi Eliezer said, "When you pray, know before Whom you stand!" (Mishnah Berakhot 4:4)[16]

The truth is that Jews were seriously trying to get in touch with God. As the realization of the necessity of working at prayer hits us, almost everything about our prayer life will change—our posture, our focus, our volume, everything! For myself, when I learned to pray, I determined, *I'm going to be a spiritual athlete. I'm going to get up off the chair.* Why? Because I fall asleep sitting there! Now I move around when I pray. We teach our congregation at church to engage, to get up, to put their hands on someone and to get involved. It's hard work. "Wake up, O sleeper," Paul encourages the Ephesians, "rise from the dead, and Christ will shine on you" (Eph. 5:14). We also see it as a must for teaching beginners to use volume, because they tend to be timid in group settings. Dare we say, the more volume, the better. Why? Because volume takes energy and emotion. It's hard to have volume for any length of time if one is not into it, downcast or moody. The other day I was teaching at a school of prayer and prophecy for a week. I got up one morning for the preservice prayer, feeling somewhat lonely and out of it. Verses about the angels crying out with a loud voice in the presence of God were running through my head, but frankly, I felt more like sitting down and saying nothing. Nevertheless, as I began to walk around, I forced myself to shout the Word of God up to His throne. Within seconds, I was not only into my prayers, but the rest of the class was as well. Passion begets passion—just like David's dance (see 2 Sam. 6:14-15). It is also part of what is meant by loving and worshiping with all of our strength and soul. This is not to say that silence and solitude are invalid (see chapter 7), but rather, in the beginning stages of our prayer life, or even when we begin a specific prayer time, we must not use silent prayer and quietness as an excuse to remain passive and disconnected.

Thus, whether it is the labor of showing up consistently, forcing the mind to engage or increasing our emotional involvement, we must expect to work at prayer. In this work of prayer, Mike Bickle also encourages us to keep clear the division of labor—you will water (commune with the Lord) and weed the garden (deal with your sin), after which God will produce the life. All we can do as humans is plant, water and weed. It is God who gives the increase and it is God who produces the fruit. John 15 tells us to abide in the vine—Jesus. That is what prayer is about, remaining close to Jesus and abiding in Him. The fruit is all His doing, as is the pruning for future growth. Discipline can easily become legalism, but it doesn't have to if our prayer life simply remains a faithful labor of watering and weeding. Mike Bickle finds instructions for the weeding process in Ephesians 5 and Philippians 2:

1. Take full responsibility for your sin, calling it sin, and not blaming it on anyone or anything (see Eph. 5:3-7).

2. Don't complain. Bring complaints to God first and then to another person only if He gives you permission (see Phil. 2:14).

3. Submit to each other: spouse, children, jobs, church, government and so on (see Eph. 5:22-33).

All of this, as we know, is hard work. And all of the watering we may attempt in our devotional time and in our lives may be futile unless we also do the daily weeding in the garden of sanctification.

WE NEED TO PRAY IN SECRET

Last, most of the work of prayer has to be done in secret. Prayer is one of the four disciplines, along with giving, acts of righteousness and fasting, which Jesus teaches are best done in secret. If we get public acclaim for prayers, we already have our reward. Nevertheless, we do have earthly rewards in prayer. In fact, the goal and the reward of prayer may be one and the same. For centuries, many have testified that the goal of all of the work, or structure, of prayer was to move the "interior feeling."

"Prayer without interior feeling is not very effective, either for the one who recites it or for the one who listens to it; everything depends on interior life and on attentive prayer! But how few people are occupied with interior activity! The reason for this is that they don't really want it; they have no yearning for spiritual life and interior enlightenment," says the priest in *The Way of the Pilgrim*. His people were irritated with him because he prayed so slowly and thus the service went very long. But he said, "I choose to think about every word of prayer before I vocalize it."[17]

Thomas Kelly said that "life is meant to be lived from a Center, a divine Center. Each one of us can live such a life of amazing power and peace and serenity, of integration and confidence and simplified multiplicity, on one condition—that is, if we really want to."[18] So says a man who must not only have seen the goal but also attained it and benefited from the rewards. The goal of the work of moving the heart was attained when the presence of God came. It is He who moves our hearts to tears. It is His Spirit who communicates with "groans that words cannot express" (Rom. 8:26). These are manifestations of His felt presence. This is the *pathway to spirituality*.

However, having seen the goal, we must again underscore the work that it takes to attain it. We simply want to emphasize the fact that it is going to take hard work to become a proficient prayer. This work will likely mean a change of posture (from sitting or lying down to standing and walking or rocking), a change of volume (from silent daydreaming to focused vocalization of the Bible) and a change in goal (we are out to communicate to and touch the heart of God, thereby having an interior response in our own souls). The Bible shows people standing, raising their arms, lying prostrate before the Lord (with their faces to the ground), walking, pacing, kneeling and facing Jerusalem when they prayed. It shows people (and angels) crying, shouting, sweating and intently focusing in their prayers. It shows people praying morning and afternoon, getting up early and knocking on doors in the middle of the night. We again affirm, as we did at the beginning of this chapter, that effective prayer involves work—serious work, hard work and consistent work. So gird up your loins, roll up your sleeves and get ready to do business with God.

CHAPTER THREE

PRAY EVERY DAY

Set a Time. Set a Place. And Pray Every Day.

Two busy executives meet at a company luncheon. They embrace heartily and say, "Where've you been? How're you doing?" They play rapid catch-up—the wife, the kids, the work, the latest. Desiring the connection that nurtures every friendship, one says, "We've got to get together sometime." Just as eager to enjoy the relationship, the other says, "Yeah, let's do it!" Wisely, the bolder one takes immediate initiative and says, "Let's book a time and a place right now, or it won't happen." "Okay, next week, Thursday lunch, at the old deli spot we used to go to." "Right, I'll see you then."

Without a time and a place, good intentions usually are left undone. In the words of one old sage, "at some point we have to put the pen to paper and schedule it in." We all know that life is lived in time and space. The stuff we do is accomplished sometime and somewhere! For example, last night my wife and I went to the Tower restaurant for a romantic meal. A month ago, the kids and I went fishing. On Sunday, we will go to church. Next Thanksgiving, we are all going to my parent's house. Relationships are cultivated in real time and space—quality time—where both parties are present in the moment. And even though God is everywhere and knows everything, not everyone everywhere is close to Him. Why? Because not everyone chooses to cultivate the relationship in time and space.

God desires relationship with us. Ardent believers of every age will all agree on this one point: Progress in friendship with God will require the practice of daily prayers. If God says, "Pray!" and we respond by saying, "Sure, when I get around to it," and we never actually pray, then we are disobedient, which is reminiscent of the parable of the son who said he would but did not do (see Matt. 21:28-31; Jas. 1:25). Obedience, not just desire, is critical to being doers of the Word. Spending time, talking, visiting, being in the presence of and loving each other are the building blocks of relationship and intimacy. And prayer is the practice of these building blocks—things that build relationship with God. Whether it's proclamational, devotional, intercessory, declarative or worshipful prayer, it all brings us closer to God. And they all take place in time and space.

RUNNING OUT OF TIME

So why don't we pray? Our not-so-original excuse is, I have no time! *Time* magazine even ran a cover article not so long ago entitled, "America Is Running Out of Time!" Most people feel like they have no time. Really, has there ever been enough time? Yet if we are honest, we have to admit that we have the same amount of time that Jesus had—24 hours a day. Consider the perspective of the saints of old. Martin Luther once said, "I have so much to do, I must pray three hours today." Saint Vincent de Paul prayed five or six hours daily in order to have the supernatural efficacy to do as much he did. Kevin Prosch sang, "Our time, which is precious, we pour out like oil."[1] For everyone with somewhere to go or something to do, *time* is the new costly perfume.

Given that the ancients are right when they say, "You learn to pray by praying" and that God knows that our spirits are willing, but our flesh is weak, God qualifies the general call to prayer by setting it in time and space. As we shall see, we are safe to say that throughout Scripture, the Bible commands us to discipline ourselves to specific times of daily, focused, Bible prayer.

PRAYING ACCORDING TO CUSTOM

It was Jesus' custom to pray (see chapter 2). We know that, at that time, in the custom of a Jewish boy growing up in a Jewish culture, with Jewish beliefs, He did what all righteous Jewish boys did—prayed three times a day. Joachim Jeremias writes:

> The three hours of prayer in particular were so universally observed among the Jews of Jesus' time that we are

justified in including them in the comment "as his custom was" which is made in Luke with reference to Jesus'
attendance at Sabbath worship (Luke 4:16).[2]

What's more, Jesus' whole life would have been shaped
around these set times of prayer, because the tradition of daily
prayer long predates His birth. When God led His people of
Israel out of Egypt to a place where they would freely worship
Him, He gave them His Law. Deuteronomy 6 became the central passage for all of Judaism. Rightly, the people understood
that the command given in this passage was the core of
Yahweh worship, and out of it everything else extended.
Whatever else they did, all Jews tried to obey this specific command as well as the longer Ten Commandments (see Exod.
20). Jeremias adds that:

> It is probable from the last words of this injunction,
> "and when you lie down, and when you rise", that the
> custom of beginning and ending each day with the con-
> fession of the one God is derived.[3]

As we said, boys were taught the words as soon as they could
speak. Hence, the Jews began to recite the Shema every morning
and every evening. Remember, though, that reciting the creed
was not the same as daily prayers. Every Jew was to say daily
prayers, not just the males, as in the case of the Shema. Of this,
Jeremias writes:

> There is a difference in character between the Shema and
> the *Tephilla*; as mentioned earlier, only freemen were

obliged to recite the Shema, whereas the *Tephilla* was to be said by all, including women, children, and even slaves.[4]

However, it was only a small jump to begin including prayers after the recital of the creed.

Then after Moses' time, the leadership baton was passed to Joshua. God reemphasized the pattern that he gave to Moses and reinstated the commands that He intended Joshua to carry on. In the opening verses of Joshua's call, God summarized what He wanted—namely, that His people would obey, love and trust in Him. The structure of this call is found in Joshua 1:6-9:

> Be strong and courageous, because you will lead these people to inherit the land I swore to their forefathers to give them. Be strong and very courageous. *Be careful to obey all the law my servant Moses gave you;* do not turn from it to the right or to the left, *that you may be successful wherever you go.* Do not let this *Book of the Law* depart from your mouth; *meditate on it day and night, so that you may be careful to do everything written in it. Then you will be prosperous and successful.* Have I not commanded you? Be strong and courageous. Do not be terrified; do not be discouraged, for the LORD your God will be with you wherever you go (emphasis added).

PASSING THE BATON

The point that we want to highlight in this chapter is the commitment to daily praying of the Bible or meditating on the Law *day and night.* The exegetical question is, What is meant by the phrase "day and night"? Is God really serious about having his people show up *day and night?* What are the parameters of the phrase "day and night"? Is this a religious cliché, poetic language or what? Does it really mean that we should pray 24 hours a day without ceasing, in every waking moment of our life? Or is this command merely a euphemism for something else, such as regularly or continually? God's intention in this command to Joshua should be understood primarily by two things: (1) the context in which it was given and (2) how the people who received this command lived it out.

The primary commands taken from Joshua 1:6-9 are

> Don't be afraid to obey and trust God. You will be able to do this if you meditate, that is, recite, the Book of the Law (the Holy Scriptures) to God (the direction of the meditation) day and night (every day, morning, noon and night). If you do this, then you will be able to do what I say, and I will bless and prosper you.

Paraphrasing this into a single sentence, we could interpret the command as the power to obey and trust God will come when you pray the Bible out loud to God every day!

However, before we look at this command and how it was passed down from generation to generation, let's consider how most modern men interpret this passage. Having pastored for over 20 years, we have a lot of insight on the modern-day application of this text. For starters, it is almost impossible, particularly for men, to conceive of literally praying the Law of God out loud to Him every waking minute of every day. For most, unceasing prayer is thought of as more of a special vocation for the monastic few than as a binding command for the general populace. A logical man reasons like this: God put man in the Garden to tend and domesticate it, so He obviously intended us to do more than sit around praying all day. After the Fall, God told us that we would have to live by the sweat of our brow, which entails hard work. Grow this, build that, count everything, and then show us the money! That is really what we are supposed to do. We are the basic hunter-gatherers of the created order.

If we take this line of reasoning further, we realize that the responsibility to domesticate the land also is coupled with the command to be fruitful and multiply. Ancient Jews were not in favor of monastic celibacy but celebrated life and family. From the beginning, God instituted marriage. But with marriage comes children, and now both men and women have to work twice as hard just to survive. There is a need for more food, bigger shelters, a wheel and horse to move all the stuff around and on and on. Living this sort of life has become a full-time occupation.

Thus, put the command to pray in this context and you have any logical man questioning, How can I meditate on the Law *day and night*? I can't just sit around on a rock all day praying. *Day and night* must not mean a literal *day and night*. Rather, it must just be a euphemism for "often"! And "often" is a relative term, meaning when I get around to it, which practically speaking means "never"! Ultimately, the way most normal men justify their having faith in what the Bible says while not doing anything about it is by rationalizing it away into meaninglessness.

But is it possible that God meant something other than man's logical conclusion when He gave this command? Maybe the ancient Jews in their earnest desire to actually *do* what God said were more correct than we are today in rationalizing it away.

Perhaps their interpretation of the command—to meditate on His Law *day and night,* which for them meant coming before Him at least every 12 hours (every morning and every night)—is more correct than ours. As we always say, it's hard to backslide in 12 hours.

Sad but true, our spirituality takes place in the rhythm of life. Of course, our marriage, family, work, friends and church activities all take time. And though it is possible to pray while eating our meals, working at our jobs, taking our children to school, going to their ball games, changing their diapers and so on, it is not probable. What is more probable

> GOD WANTS US TO SHOW UP EVERY MORNING AND EVERY NIGHT; IT'S HARD TO BACKSLIDE IN 12 HOURS.

is that God intended for us to have a few fixed times each day and each night—when everyone steps aside from their busy schedules—to focus directly on Him and pray. Innately, we know that we are supposed to pray daily. Most of us have vague notions of this in our heads, possibly absorbed through praying segments of the Lord's Prayer or through traditions that have come down to us through our denominational teachings, but *why* are we supposed to pray daily? Is there a biblical basis to this? Is daily prayer something that was instituted by God or man? Just where do these notions come from?

PRAYING AS A SACRIFICE

We are brought back to the exegetical question, What is meant by the phrase "day and night" as it relates to prayer? It is our thesis that the rabbis and sages of Israel interpreted the above Mosaic passages (see Exod. 20; Deut. 6; 10:12; 11:13; Josh. 1:8) as prescriptions for daily prayers. Admittedly, there was an evolution of how the Israelites got to the point of actually instituting daily prayer. Pertinent structural information from the time of Joshua to Samuel is scant—and religious life chaotic—but through careful study, a pattern is seen to develop. By the time of the New Testament, when Zechariah went into the holy of holies and "the time for the burning of incense came, *all the assembled worshipers were praying outside*" (Luke 1:10, emphasis added). This is a very important point that cannot be overlooked. What is not so obvious at first glance is that by the time of Jesus, prayer, in the Jewish culture, had taken on a sacrificial aspect. Prayer had become a *sacrifice* of the Jews.

Then, after the destruction of the Temple in A.D. 70, prayer replaces the sacrificial system and *becomes* the sacrifice. When Jews no longer had a temple to go to where they could offer sacrifice, prayers became their sacrificial work with all the nuances of sacrifice, atonement, propitiation and relationship. And while we reject outright that prayers are propitious as a merit of good works, we do accept that prayers are a spiritual sacrifice (see Heb. 13:15), just as mercy is (see Rom. 12:1). In other words, it is an offering. Paul even called his life a drink offering (see Phil. 2:17). It's not a works offering that merits your salvation, but it is an offering of the heart. Even so, in the Old Testament, the New Testament and beyond, we cannot get away from the fact that prayer was linked to sacrifice.

In any case, to the Jewish world, the daily sacrifice of prayer was a given—a matter of fact. How early this practice started is unknown, but a sacrifice of prayer, similar to Zechariah's sacrifice, also is recorded as early as Moses' time. The record states that when Moses would go into the tent of meeting to talk to God, all of the Israelites worshiped at the entrance of their own tents (see Exod. 33:8-10). In order to understand why this is significant, we have to look at the backdrop of this event for a moment. God had commanded Moses to erect a Tabernacle and institute the sacrifices and offerings. The "keepers of the fire" were told in no uncertain terms, "the fire must be kept burning on the altar continuously; it must not go out" (Lev. 6:13). The fires were used to consume the morning and evening sacrifices. But more than just offering up morning and evening sacrifices, God also told Moses:

Aaron must burn fragrant incense on the altar *every morning* when he tends the lamps. He must burn incense again *when he lights* the *lamps at twilight* so incense will burn *regularly* before the LORD for the generations to come (Exod. 30:7-8, emphasis added).

The imagery of the sacrifice and incense is clear. The sacrifices pointed to Jesus' future death on the cross, and the incense was symbolic of our prayer and worship to God. We know this because over a thousand years later when John was able to peer into the heavenly throne room, he "saw a Lamb, looking as if it had been slain" (Rev. 5:6). As he continued to watch:

The four living creatures and the twenty-four elders fell down before the Lamb. Each one had a harp and they were holding *golden bowls full of incense, which are the prayers of the saints* (Rev. 5:8, emphasis added).

Just as the shedding of blood in animal sacrifice was symbolic of Jesus' blood being spilled, so also the incense used for the Mosaic offerings was an earthly representation of a spiritual reality—that of prayer. Even David understood this when he sang:

> May my *prayer* be set before you like *incense*; may the *lifting up* of *my hands* be like the *evening sacrifice* (Ps. 141:2, emphasis added).

He had it exactly. The parallelism is plain: prayer and worship—*the lifting up of our hands*—is *our* daily, morning and evening offering. David was saying that this prayer is his *incense*; this worship is his *sacrifice*. And although the people were not allowed to go into the tent to offer up sacrifice with the Levites, they did what they were allowed to do. They took part by offering up daily prayers. These daily prayers coincided with the incense and animal sacrifices. Thus, it is if very early in the life of Israel, daily prayers were on the way to becoming the people's sacrifice.

> BY THE TIME OF JESUS, DAILY PRAYERS HAD BECOME THE PEOPLE'S SACRIFICE.

DAVID AND HIS TABERNACLE

As we move toward the end of the era known as the Judges, God raises up a shepherd king—David. By observing David's enthusiastic worship, we see an even clearer picture develop of how the commands of God were interpreted. Obviously David had a very thorough knowledge of the Law. According to his own testimony, he says that he gleaned this knowledge from his practice of meditating on the Law *day and night* (see Pss. 1:2; 55:17; 119:164). It's probable that he as a child was led in this practice by his parents, and they carried it on into his teenage years. In any case, the first time David appears as a teenager, he is already known for being skilled on the harp and for singing the "Song of the Lord" (see 1 Sam. 16:14-23; 18:10). As a mere youth, his knowledge of who God is emboldened him to fight a bear and a lion (see 1 Sam. 17:34-37). His courage came from the fact that he meditates on—recites and prays—the Law *day and night*. From biblical or historical exegesis, we cannot say that such prayer is a required religious duty at this point. What we can say is that daily prayer is David's common practice—the testimony of his own mouth—which he does faithfully to give expression to the holy intentions of his heart. And in David's life, this practice brought about extraordinary results from what could have been very ordinary life.

When David turns 37 years old, he is established as king over all of Judah and Israel. He now has the money, the power and the fame to do whatever he wants. In his possession is much more than today's equivalent of the 10-million-dollar lottery. Whatever he wants to do, he can do; he is the king. What would you do if you were him? What would be your ultimate dream? Amazingly, David's main desire is to bring the ark of the Lord to Jerusalem and place it on the grounds of his palace (see 1 Chron. 13:3). David knows that the ark is for the contact point that mediates the presence of God. Since he is saturated in the story of Moses, David knows how God works. He remembers that it is written:

> Make this tabernacle and all its furnishings exactly like
> the pattern I will show you. Have them make a chest of
> acacia wood. There, above the cover between the two
> cherubim that are over the ark of the Testimony, *I will
> meet with you and give you all my commands for the Israelites*
> (Exod. 25:9-10,22, emphasis added).

The whole of the Tabernacle of Moses is about God meeting with a man and talking to him *face-to-face,* as a *man speaks with his friend* (see Exod. 30:36; 33:11). Moses himself says that when he "entered the Tent of Meeting to speak with the LORD, he heard the voice speaking to him from between the two cherubim above the atonement cover on the ark of the Testimony. And he [God] spoke with him" (Num. 7:89). From this place, from between the two cherubim—about two feet square—God speaks and gives Moses the entire Law (see Lev. 1—7).

IN ESSENCE, WHAT DAVID WANTS IS GOD IN HIS OWN BACKYARD.

David thought that if he could get the ark of the Lord into a tent as Moses did, then maybe God would talk to him as He talked to Moses. Maybe God would even manifest Himself before Israel as He did in Moses' day (see Exod. 40:35-38). Maybe God would come down in fire as He did then (see Exod. 40:38; Lev. 10:2). In essence, what David wants is *God in his own backyard.*

After retrieving the ark and placing it safely in the tent on his palace grounds, David establishes what he thinks will make God happy. It is important to mention that the sacrifices of burnt offerings were not practiced in David's Tabernacle during those 33 years in Jerusalem, but rather at a different Tabernacle of the Lord at the high place in Gibeon (see 1 Chron. 16:39-43). It is only after the Temple is built by Solomon that the ark is again brought together in the same place where the animal sacrifices are offered. David's Tabernacle is, strictly speaking, a prayer and worship thing (i.e., no animal sacrifices are performed). This is important, because again we see how prayer is already taking on a sacrificial tone even at this early stage. As soon as David has the ark in his backyard:

> He appointed some of the Levites *to minister* before the ark of the LORD, *to make petition, to give thanks, and to praise* the LORD, the God of Israel: Asaph was the chief, Zechariah second, then. . . . They were to play the lyres and harps, Asaph was to sound the cymbals, and Benaiah and Jahaziel the priests were to blow the trumpets regularly before the ark of the covenant of God (1 Chron. 16:4-6, emphasis added).

THE MESSAGE puts it this way:

> That was the day that David inaugurated regular worship of praise to GOD, led by Asaph and his company (1 Chron. 16:4-6).

Obviously, David wants to do what he believes God will like. This is why he appoints groups of people *to minister daily (sharath)* before the ark, which means "to attend, serve, or wait on"; *to make petition (zakar)*, which means "to be mindful by recounting and recording, and then causing what is remembered to be continually thought upon"; *to give thanks (yadah),* which means "literally from holding out the hand, or to throw or shoot at or away"—hence, it came to be associated with worship as the extending or throwing up of the hands, to confess or shoot up thanks; and finally, *to praise the Lord (halal),* from which we get the word "hallelujah." Originally, *praise (halel)* came from a primitive root word, which meant "to be clear of sound, or more usually of color." It eventually metamorphosed into "to shine," where the word came to be associated with worship and took on the idea of deity-boasting with outrageous celebration.[5]

David hires professionals who will come into the tent to record and recount all the great things God has done. Like sports commentators who recount all the great plays or singers of ballads who immortalize heroic acts, these Levites boasted in the glory of God. They boasted so much that they caused everybody who heard them to do the same. So strong were the feelings that their zakar produced that everyone present could not help but throw their arms up in thanksgiving and praise. Like a man who shines his car or a warrior who shines his sword, David is sure that he is making the face of Yahweh more visible and more colorful than any other god. The result is electric! The people cannot keep their arms down. The people begin to praise (halel) Yahweh through prayer, song and dance until it is unleashed in wild abandon. Yahweh becomes more colorful and attractive than all the other competing gods. With this bold demonstration of who Yahweh is, David hopes that all people will break out in outrageous worship and celebration just like his team on the hill. Then, perhaps, David's secret desire of attracting the manifest presence of the Lord will materialize. Like Moses, David wants to see God's face (see Ps. 27:8).

Ultimately, David's dream becomes a reality. God does begin to show up and speak directly to him. David says that the de-tails for the courts of the Temple are put into his mind directly by the Spirit (see 1 Chron. 28:12). David also experiences a type of infused writing as the hand of the Lord comes upon him. He is moved as the Spirit gives him understanding in all of the details of the plan for the Temple (see 1 Chron. 28:19). More than that, God manifests Himself in front of all of Israel, just like in the days of Moses. As Solomon finishes dedicating the Temple, millions of common people gasp when they see fire coming down from heaven—burning up the sacrifice—followed by the glory of God above the Temple. In unison, all the people fall on the pavement, faces to the ground, as they worship and give thanks to God (see 2 Chron. 7:1-3). All this comes about because one man started the daily practice of ministering to the Lord.

The evidence of a rigorous commitment to daily prayer doesn't stop with David. It also is seen in the lives of the prophets. The compilers of the book of Kings are intent on pointing out that it is at the time of the *evening sacrifice,* while Elijah the prophet is *praying,* that he experiences his great power encounter. It reads:

> At the time of [the evening] sacrifice, the prophet Elijah stepped forward and *prayed.* Then the fire of the LORD fell and burned up the sacrifice, the wood, the stones and the soil, and also licked up the water in the trench. When all the people saw this, they fell prostrate and cried, "The LORD—he is God! The LORD—he is God!" (1 Kings 18:36,38-39).

Further, the prophet Daniel is also in the habit of doing daily prayers. His life of prayer is another major Old Testament model of what the Jews believed and, hence, lived in regard to prayer.

DANIEL AND HIS DAILY PRAYER

As the pivotal holy man who carried the Jews through their Babylonian captivity, Daniel continued to model the holy pattern. Carrying on his habit of daily prayer to a point of obsession, Daniel refused to break his habit of praying three times daily, even under the threat of death by lions. The chronicler says:

> *Three times a day he got down on his knees and prayed,* giving thanks to his God, *just as he had done before* (Dan. 6:10, emphasis added).

This 70-year practice of thrice daily prayer was something we can assume Daniel brought with him from his home in Jerusalem. It was the habit of the home that spirited the resolve of this young slave—of 14 to 15 years—to not bend to the ways of Babylon (see Dan. 1:8). Without it, who knows whether Daniel would have had the resolve to become the counterculture personality that he was. In fact, Daniel took his faith so seriously that he went to the extremes of being countercultural—in his denial of rich foods and in his adherence to a Nazarite diet of basic vegetables. Ironically, it was Daniel's worshipful lifestyle in his first year at King Nebuchadnezzar's training that led to his life being spared one year later (see Dan. 1—2).

Soon after arriving in Babylon, Daniel and his three teenage friends were forced to make their stand for God. Less than one year later, they were faced with an edict by the king, stating that all magicians, wise men, psychics and so on would be killed if they could not tell the king the interpretation of his dream (see Dan. 2:1-6). Daniel happened to be amongst the group condemned to die. Yet because of his previous stand for God and his lifestyle of prayer, Daniel was in place to seek God for a miracle. Thankfully for him and his friends, this decision of prayer and devotion turned out to be the habit that ended up saving their lives (see Dan. 2:17-49). From that point on, we see that at every point of testing, the maturity of Daniel's spiritual life and the faith he cultivated through the habit of daily prayer carried him to the pinnacle of power.

Another observation concerning daily prayer in Daniel's life was seen in the way his prayers coincided with the daily sacrifice. Near the end of his life, Daniel said:

> I, Daniel, understood from the Scriptures, according to the word of the LORD given to Jeremiah the prophet, that the desolation of Jerusalem would last seventy years. So I turned to the Lord God and pleaded with him in prayer and petition, in fasting, and in sackcloth and ashes (Dan. 9:2-3).

Daniel enters into a serious fast for the fulfillment of Israel's return from captivity. The prayer in Daniel 9 becomes a model for national repentance and revival. From the text, we are not told how long Daniel prayed and fasted, but the inference was that it was many days. Interestingly enough, while the fasting is continual, the set times of prayer are still observed. The text records that the most famous messenger angel—Gabriel—"came to me in swift flight about the time of *the evening sacrifice*" (Dan. 9:21, emphasis added). Why? Because that's when Daniel was praying. The evening sacrificial time coincided with the third prayer watch of Daniel's day. Not only did Daniel receive the answer concerning the crisis, but he also received one of the most significant prophecies in the Old Testament concerning the coming of Messiah (see Dan. 9:20-27). All of these noteworthy events happened during scheduled prayer times.

EZRA AND THE ESTABLISHMENT OF SET TIMES OF PRAYER

After the exiles began to return from Babylon in 539 B.C. under the leadership of Zerubbabel, the rebuilding process of the Temple began. For hundreds of years, the prophets had exhorted the people to love the Lord, to maintain temple worship and not to forsake their religious obligations. The people didn't listen, and the severe punishment of captivity was the result. Now, having returned from Babylon, the people were again losing interest in their main purpose for returning—rebuilding the Temple and reestablishing Yahweh worship. When Ezra, the scribe, visited Jerusalem, he was horrified. He responded by going into a time of prayer and fasting. Evidently, it was his prayer at *the evening sacrifice* (see Ezra 9:4-15) that led to another national revival. From this point on, historians tell us that Ezra resolved that Israel would never again provoke God to such wrath. Ezra acted out of deep conviction and reinforced the practice of daily prayers, accompanied with readings from the Torah. Eventually, daily prayers became normative in the Jewish culture (c. 450 B.C.).

Jewish expert George Robinson writes:

Group public prayer in Judaism probably dates from the early days of the Second Temple, around 400 B.C.E. These early prayer services, which were held in addition to, and possibly in conjunction with, sacrifices and offerings, are believed to have included the Shema, some Psalms, and *in lieu of sacrifices at certain times*, Torah readings.

Many of the practices that we associate with Jewish worship today date far back to this period. Ezra is believed to have begun the reading of the Torah in the public square in Jerusalem over four hundred years B.C.E. Regular readings would take place on Mondays and Thursdays, the market days during which men and women would gather to trade and sell; today, the weekday morning services at which the Torah is read still takes place on Mondays and Thursdays. Many of the prayers that we still read today date from this period.[6]

Of daily prayer, Jeremias points out that from the Temple cult (of Solomon), there arose another order of rank-and-file priests and Levites who served in the Temple but were not permanent residents. These extras were called the standing posts, and they were scattered over the whole of Israel. After the exile (after Ezra's time), when the twenty-four courses of established representatives would go up to Jerusalem for their week of service, a corresponding number or lay group would stay back in their towns during its priestly course's week of service. The ones who remained behind assembled in the synagogue to read the Scriptures and pray, so as to participate in the Temple service from a distance. This was called the standing posts.

There can be no doubt that it was above all the members of the Pharisaic groups who volunteered to serve in the "standing posts" and to pray in lieu of the people of their district. Presumably the Pharisees, too, were responsible for extending the prayers said daily by the "standing posts" during their week of service over the whole year. They probably also extended the obligation of saying the Tephilla to all members of household, including women, children, and slaves.[7]

The development of daily prayers came and took their place alongside what was happening in the Temple. To repeat what we said before, our thesis is to show that daily prayer had become the people's sacrifice, which is evident by this time.

During the 400 years from Ezra on, it became customary for all Jews to pray the Eighteen Benedictions, coupled with readings from the Torah, over three set *hours* of prayer at the temple, synagogue or home. This custom was firmly in place long before the birth of Jesus. Accordingly, Jesus, along with every righteous Jew, would have observed this daily practice. As mentioned earlier, Jesus, his father Joseph and Joseph's father would have prayed this way according to the custom of the day. Peter, James and John grew up praying set prayers every day. Saul, the strict Pharisee, was steeped in the model of Jewish prayer. In other words, there was an existing culture of prayer that the Early Church was born into. And since the New Testament Church was made up almost entirely of devout Jews who practiced Jewish Old Testament prayer, it would have never occurred to them to challenge it.

JESUS AND DAILY PRAYER

By the time Jesus and His disciples entered the scene, they were trying to correct the abuses of their day (see Matt. 6:5-18; 23:5-7), all the while reinforcing the important practice of daily, scheduled prayer (see Matt. 23:23; Luke 18:1-14; 19:46). In Matthew 6:5-15, Jesus reacted not to the number or routine of these prayers, but to the showy manner of those praying. Alms, prayers and fasting had become traditions devoid of passion and reality and were nothing more than pretentious religious displays. Jesus began to encourage His disciples to pray in private, as an antidote to the vain repetition of public prayers, which were said only to be seen by men. Yes, it was true that the Temple was the official *place* of prayer, but in order to ward off hypocrisy, it was much better if the show-offs just prayed at home—in secret—and then the Father who sees in secret would be able to reward them openly (see Matt. 6:6). In essence, Jesus was saying that prayer done in a nonholy place, but with a holy heart, was more valid than prayer done "right" in a so-called sacred spot. In all of His correctives, however, Jesus never promoted the idea that routine prayer was to be abandoned, that people should only pray when the Spirit moved them or that the daily set times of prayer were part of the old wineskin.

What is of critical importance to us is that most evangelical/charismatic Christians do not believe that the New Testament actually endorses and continues the Old Testament practice of daily prayer. Consequently, they do not fully expect the practice to be carried on in our day. For Jesus, even His correctives were all about continuing to do daily prayer, but doing it with the right motive and attitude. Joachim Jeremias states:

We may conclude with all probability that no day in the life of Jesus passed without the three times of prayer: the morning prayer at sunrise, the afternoon prayer at the time when the afternoon sacrifice was offered in the Temple, the evening prayer at night before going to sleep.[8]

Jesus' parables on prayer were to teach his disciples that "they should always pray and not give up" (Luke 18:1). Jesus even quotes the "day and night" phrase that the Old Testament linked to prayer. He said, "God [will] bring about [speedy] justice for his chosen ones, who cry out to Him *day and night*" (Luke 18:7, emphasis added). Jesus modeled prayer as a lifestyle. From all of what Jesus taught and did, His message on prayer is clear: To get where you want to be, you have to keep on praying the Bible out loud to God every day.

DAILY PRAYER IN THE EARLY CHURCH

The model of prayer becomes even more clear and more substantial when we look into the history of the Early Church. No longer is the prayer model a thing of conjecture, formed out of biographical customs or interpretations of isolated texts. The evidence from the New Testament is that the Early Church not only accepted the tradition of *day and night* prayer but also reinforced it. After Jesus rose from the dead, He told His disciples to go and pray until they got what He would be sending them. The last verse of the Gospel of Luke reads:

And they stayed *continually* at the temple, praising God (Luke 24:53, emphasis added).

PRAY EVERY DAY   87

This concept of "staying continually" at the temple courts in Acts becomes critical to the understanding of daily prayer. As the early disciples prayed through the 10 days before the out-pouring of Pentecost, Luke highlights that they were "constant-ly in prayer" (Acts 1:14). Then on Pentecost at *the third hour* (9:00 A.M.)—coming out of the early morning time of prayer (see Acts 2:15)—the Holy Spirit fell. Imagine that—the initial outpouring of the Holy Spirit came out of a set, organized and predicted time of prayer!

The practices of the Church born at Pentecost are clearly delineated in the book of Acts. The Scriptures say:

> And they were *continually devoting themselves* to the apos-tles' teaching and to fellowship, to the breaking of bread and *to prayer*. And *day by day continuing* with one mind *in the temple* (Acts 2:42,46, *NASB,* emphasis added).

The Greek words Luke uses—in a row—emphasize devotion in prayer. The words are: *eesan de proskarterontes,* which mean "they continued steadfastly and they continued steadfastly." Vine's dic-tionary says the root, *proskartereo,* means "to be strong towards (*pros* means 'towards,' used intensively, and *kartereo* means 'to be strong'), to endure in, or persevere in, to be continually steadfast with a person or thing." It's "continuing" in prayer with others.[9]

Therefore, when the disciples were daily in the temple courts, what were they doing? Jesus said they were praying. With fury, he thundered:

> My house [the temple] will be called a *house of prayer* for all nations (Mark 11:17, emphasis added).

In another parable, Jesus again states why people went to the temple. "Two men went up to the temple *to pray*" (Luke 18:10, emphasis added). Jesus tells us where they prayed. They went "up to the temple to pray!" Understanding this point alone will change the way we have interpreted the New Testament. For years, we have heard that the Church met daily in the temple courts and from house to house. The interpretation normally given—from North American pulpits at least—is that the Church enjoyed corporate celebration with worship and teaching at the temple, after which they went from house to house enjoying more Bible study, fellowship and communion. However, this is simply wrong! They did not go to the temple for good corporate gatherings. They went up to the temple to pray! The Early Church was not celebrating or "gossiping the gospel" in the temple courts. Instead, they were *praying*—daily and continually—fulfilling the customary hours of prayer. Whatever else they did by way of teaching, visiting and fellowship, it did not preclude the practice of daily prayer.

Furthermore, daily prayer is what the primitive Church continued to model. Luke is keen to point this out:

> Peter and John were going up to the temple at the ninth hour, *the hour of prayer* (Acts 3:1, *NASB,* emphasis added).

Without a doubt, the apostles *continued* to observe the set hours of prayer. When the ministry increased to the point that they were becoming too busy to pray, the apostles called for a time-out:

It would not be right for us to neglect the ministry of the word of God in order to wait on tables. Brothers, choose seven men from among you who are known to be full of the Spirit and wisdom. We will turn this responsibility over to them and will give our attention to *prayer* and *the ministry of the word* (Acts 6:2-4, emphasis added).

In other words, they delegated some responsibilities in order to go back to the practice of daily prayer, along with the "ministry of the word."

Commendation for continuous prayer can be found in Scripture as well. Cornelius, a Gentile God-fearer, is called a devout man who prayed continually or regularly (see Exod. 30:8). The regularity of his prayer was reminiscent of the command to Moses that incense is to be burned regularly before the Lord, every morning and evening.

About the ninth hour of the day [the hour of prayer] he clearly saw in a vision an angel of God who had just come in to him, and said to him, "Cornelius!" . . . "Your prayers and alms have ascended as a memorial before God" (Acts 10:3-4, *NASB*).

Cornelius was commended for his continual prayer, that is, his daily, regimented, set times of prayer. There probably were days when Cornelius felt like he was just grinding it out in the daily routine of his scheduled prayer time. But God affirmed His delight in Cornelius's practice of daily prayers by sending an angel to tell Cornelius that these very *prayers* and *alms* have gone up to heaven and have built a memorial before the presence of

God. The word "memorial" in the Greek is *mnemosunon,* from which we get the words "reminder" or "memorandum" (i.e., a record, hence a memorial).[10] This is the same word Jesus used to commend Mary of Bethany when she poured expensive perfume on His feet. He said:

YOUR DAILY PRAYERS ARE LIKE MEMOS OF COSTLY PERFUME THAT RISE TO HEAVEN TO REMIND GOD OF YOU!

Assuredly, I say to you, wherever this gospel is preached in the whole world, what this woman has done will also be told as a *memorial* to her (Matt. 26:13, *NKJV,* emphasis added).

Do you understand what this means to God? Your daily prayers are like memos of costly perfume that rise to heaven to remind God of you!

We know of virtually no one today who equates the call to *continual prayer* (see Acts 1:14; 2:42,46; 6:4; Rom. 12:12; Col. 4:2; 1 Thess. 1:3; 2:13; 5:17; Heb. 13:15) as a call to regular, daily prayer. Again, we quote the words of Joachim Jeremias:

When Paul says that he prays "continually," "without ceasing," "day and night" and "always," we are not to think of uninterrupted praying but of his observance of the regular hours of prayer. The phrase "to be instant in prayer" (*proskarterein* Rom. 12:12; Col. 4:2) is to be understood in a similar way, for *proskarterein* here means "faithfully to observe a rite" (as in Acts 1:14; 2:46; 6:4).[11]

UNDERSTANDING THE SIGNIFICANCE OF DAILY PRAYER

Now that the long-awaited Messiah had finally come, why would it occur to the followers of fulfilled Judaism to abandon daily prayer? Unlike the requirements of the Law, prayer was not in contradiction to the sacrificial work of Jesus. No, it was the means to attaining a mature faith.

The Didache (meaning "the Teaching") is perhaps the oldest noncanonical New Testament document. In its introduction to what is universally accepted as the writings of the *The Apostolic Fathers,* the editors say:

> The Didache may have been put into its present form as late as 150, though a date considerably closer to the end of the first century seems more probable. The materials from which it was composed, however, reflect the state of the church at an even earlier time. In his very thorough commentary, J. P. Audet suggests about A.D. 70, and he is not likely to be off by more than a decade in either direction.[12]

The Didache summarizes the expectations of the faithful emerging from the actual time of the apostles. In section 8, the Didache states:

> But do not let your fasts coincide with those of the hypocrites [presumably a reference to the Jews]. They fast on Monday and Thursday, so you must fast on Wednesday and Friday. (2) Nor should you pray like the hypocrites.

Instead, "pray like this," just as the Lord commanded in his Gospel: [the Lord's Prayer follows]. (3) Pray like this three times a day.[13]

The main point of this early discovery is that while the second generation Gentile Church was moving away from its Jewish moorings—due to its hostility toward the unbelieving Jews and the Jewish contents of the prayers (as mentioned in chapter 2)—they continued to stress and adhere to the practices of daily prayer and weekly fasting.

In his *Search for the Origins of Christian Worship*, Paul Bradshaw maintains that daily times of prayer form an unbroken transition from the Old to the New Testaments. He quotes the earliest sources, proving that it was the clear intent of the Early Church fathers that every believer should engage in set times of prayer every day. Clement of Alexandria and Origen spoke of praying three times a day and again at night, while:

The Western writers such as Tertullian and Cyprian record five set times of prayer a day—morning, third hour, sixth hour (noon), ninth hour, and evening—together with prayer at night.[14]

The conclusion is this:

The oldest Christian pattern of daily prayer seems to have been threefold—morning, noon, and evening—together with prayer at night. . . . Threefold daily prayer was indeed widespread, if not a universal, custom in the early Church, whether structured according to the natural rhythm of the day—praying morning, noon, and evening—or adopting the major divisions of the day in the Roman Empire at third, sixth, and ninth hours. These two traditions seem later to have been conflated into the fivefold pattern that we first encounter in third-century Africa.[15]

Even the relative newcomer Islam testifies to the unquestionable commonality of daily prayer, since Islam actually borrowed from the prevalent religious practices of the Jews and Christians. The pillars on which Muhammad founded Islam were not new or unique. They were direct copies of the disciplines that Jews and Christians had observed for hundreds of years, such as:

1. Reciting the creed (see Deut. 6:4);
2. Praying five times a day according to the citywide call to prayer (standard—see Matt. 6:5);
3. Praying Scripture (see Josh. 1:8; Eph. 5:19);
4. Praying while facing the holy place (see 2 Chron. 6:20,38; Dan. 6:10);
5. Washing and prostration (standard);
6. Almsgiving (see Prov. 19:17; Dan. 4:27; Matt. 6:1-4);
7. Walking around the prayer site in groups (temple or monasteries);
8. Fasting (see Matt. 6:16-18);
9. Pilgrimaging.

These were all well-established Christian practices, and most of them had existed in some form or another in Judaism at least

1,000 years before Islam. It is ironic that Muslims now do out of legalism what we Christians won't do in grace—that is, pray!

So we submit to you that daily prayer is not just a good idea, the latest program or most popular Christian fad. Daily prayer is not just something that the really committed intercessors do. No, daily, regulated prayer is the pattern established by God so that the first commandment becomes first place. Set times of daily prayer will enable us to love God with all of our heart, soul, strength and mind. Jesus called this "the first and greatest commandment" (Matt. 22:38). If we really want to be like Jesus, or Mary, John the Baptist, Peter, James or John, then we need to do what they did. We need to pray the Law, the Psalms, other parts of the Bible and our own benedictions, out loud, to God, two or three times every day. The location we choose to pray doesn't matter, because now our bodies are the temple of the Holy Spirit (see 1 Cor. 3:16). The fact that we show up—wherever it may be—is what really matters.

> THE MORE WE MISS THE STIRRINGS, THE LESS THEY COME. THE DULLER WE ARE, THE DULLER WE BECOME. IN THE END, IT WILL NOT BE A STIRRING THAT CALLS US TO PRAYER BUT A CRISIS.

Unfortunately, in many of our churches, there is no history or tradition of daily prayer—either on an individual or corporate level. We prefer to wait to pray until we feel inspired. *The Cloud of Unknowing* labels these interior invitations from the Holy Spirit to prayer as "touches of God."[16] These touches of

God, or stirrings, are unpredictable drawings from God, calling us to be with Him. While these stirrings are beautiful and greatly desired, they are not to be relied upon as our main motivations for prayer. Some fear that if they pray at scheduled times of prayer—even when they don't really feel like it—it would be phony or legalistic. While that is possible, the alternative is that if you don't pray until you feel like it, you most likely will not pray at all—and it won't be long until you're cold and dead. Why? Because flesh so rarely feels inspired. And the more we miss the stirrings, the less they come. The duller we are, the duller we become. In the end, it will not be a stirring that calls us to prayer but a crisis. As for us, we never wait for stirrings or inspiration. Like Smith Wigglesworth, who used to say, "I begin in the flesh and I end in the spirit," we go ahead and start praying "in the flesh." Experience bears out that we are usually moved by the Spirit when the Spirit is already moving in us. Even if you don't feel like it, do it anyway. Book a time and meet with God.

WHY SHOULD WE PRAY EVERY DAY?

Having established much historical and biblical proof as to why we are called to institute daily prayer as the *pathway to spirituality,* the question remains, Why or what will happen if I don't? How does praying daily at scheduled times relate to loving God? It could be said that daily prayer invites us daily to the table of the Lord so that we may eat of Him. Jesus said:

> It is written: "Man does not live on bread alone, but on every word that comes from the mouth of God" (Matt. 4:4).

Prayer sets us in a place to feed on the Word of God and to receive revelation from God. It fills and at the same time creates a great hunger for spirituality—for the presence of God.

Apart from God, our spirits shrivel and our carnal appetites grow out of control. Look at secular society as it lives by the attitude, Eat, drink and be merry, for tomorrow we die. Matthew Henry makes the statement:

> If there is no resurrection then our faith is in vain and so we may as well live like beasts if we are going to die like them.[17]

Henry's assertion is that without faith in God, people often live like beasts because they are following their basic urges. During New Testament times—as in our own—the prevalent cultural attitude of pagans had infected the Church to such an extent that sex was seen as just like eating—as meat for the body. Just as meat is for the belly and the belly for meat, so pleasuring oneself with a prostitute was seen as no different than eating a hamburger. Paul contradicted such an attitude and encouraged the Corinthians to elevate their sights far above their basic urges:

> The body is not for fornication, but for the Lord (1 Cor. 6:13, KJV).

We need to hear this loud and clear today. Fallen man is prone to spending most of his time, energy and money on the basic physical and psychological urges. If one were actually to try to calculate the time, energy and money that goes into servicing the appetite as society encourages, most of us would be shocked. As evidenced by the media, everyone is eating, sex is in your face and people everywhere are getting drunk or drugged up. The market vies for your last dollar in exchange for more subtle pleasures, whether they be the latest fashion, the hottest hot tub, the fastest car, tickets to the games, a better house or the ultimate fantasy getaway. Imagine how much of our world revolves around this. It could be said that this *is* what most of society goes to work for. All classes of society—whether it's the blue-collar worker at the factory waiting for the weekend to go drink beer with his buddies, the college kid studying and binging or the well-dressed executive with the best of everything—all are searching for pleasure.

HOW CAN WE COMBAT THESE PERVASIVE SOCIETAL MIND-SETS?

Daily prayer was given by God to help us order our affections and desires appropriately. The ancient Israelites are a case in point. God dictated their eating habits by distinguishing kosher (clean) and nonkosher (unclean) foods. Many of these dietary laws had direct health benefits, but another main effect was how it impacted their social life. What one ate determined who one ate with. Mixing at the fellowship table with the rest of the nonkosher world became all but impossible. Every time a Jew ate, he knew whom he served. Not only what he ate, but also when he did not eat was important. Special times of fasting were introduced by God as a spiritual discipline in order to get us in touch with what it is like to have mastery over our basic urges.

Second, God demanded a culture of holiness with respect to sexuality. Beginning with the circumcision of Abraham and continuing with a whole list of holy and unholy sexual practices—including prohibitions on fornication (see Lev. 20), adultery (see Exod. 20:14; Lev. 20:10; Deut. 5:18), homosexuality (see Lev. 20:13) and voyeurism (see Lev. 18:10-18)—God set His people apart from the rest. The Law even went so far as to prescribe when it was clean to engage in sexual relations (see Lev. 18:19). For example, it prescribed how many days it was to be before a husband could be intimate with his wife after her menstrual cycle (see Lev. 15:19-26). If this command was followed faithfully, it would've meant that most couples would be engaging in intimate relations at about the time when a woman was able to conceive and become pregnant.[18] The results were obvious: lots of children. And more children have a way of creating responsibility in a family. In this way, sexuality was encouraged within the proper setting of love and commitment.

Last, within the rhythm of everyday life, the Israelites stopped everything they were doing three times a day to focus directly on God in prayer. They also observed a weekly Sabbath to set aside time for God, self and family. In this way, God became a daily focus of the whole culture. The lifestyle of the average Israelite was set around observing the commands of God. As God captured their attention, He ultimately attracted their hearts. By influencing the nation in regard to the basic handling of food, sex and time, God discipled a people into loving and following Him.

HOW CAN WE BE SURE DAILY PRAYER IS VALID?

The effects of just one of the above disciplines—daily prayer—has had a profound influence on shaping Western civilization. After the initial discipline of the Early Church fathers began to wane, the monks of the fifth century started a countercultural prayer movement where they would practice *day and night* prayer.

Fleeing the cities (and even the churches), they founded small enclaves where they could flee from the lust of the eye, the lust of the flesh and the pride of life. In the desert, these monks gave themselves fully to the "Work of God" (the *opre diem*)—that is, they worked and prayed. Over the next 1,000 years, what began as a countercultural movement to shape one's life around prayer actually succeeded. It kept spirituality alive on the continent and ultimately gave birth to what we know as Western civilization.

The thesis of Thomas Cahill's *How the Irish Saved Civilization* is that the Roman Empire fell, as did all of Europe, to unwashed barbarians who looted artifacts, burned books and generally destroyed the transition from Greco-Roman to Judeo-Christian cultures as it was transmitted to Europe. After that, the lot fell to an army of Irish monks and scribes who single-handedly refound European civilization's history, and most important, its religion. They did this because they believed certain beliefs and held certain values born out of *day and night* prayer that they practiced in the monasteries. They had the only safe supply of books, history and records. With almost playful zeal, they wrote, transcribed, taught and rebuilt that which was destroyed. Thus, it was praying Irish monks—more than any other segment of society—who helped facilitate the Christian transition from classical to medieval Europe. In this way, all of Europe—in essence—came under the tutorage of a culture that built itself around daily prayer.[19]

With the industrial revolution, and especially with the introduction of electricity, the rhythms and patterns of mankind were changed forever. More than any other, the invention of electricity succeeded in canceling the difference between *day and night,* hot and cold, light and dark. For millennia, civilizations had to work with nature—harvest in the summer to prepare for the winter, get up when it was light and go to bed when it was dark. Benedict, for instance, wanted his monks to eat their meals by daylight so that they did not need the lamp to eat (*Rule* 41). The implication was that the monks went to sleep at 7 P.M. and got their seven hours of sleep so that they were able to rise again at 2 A.M. Benedict had his monks rise for prayer not much later than today's TV-viewers go to bed.

On a practical note:

Benedict seems to have wanted his monks to see the coming of day in this light (that of dawn and sunrise as being like the day coming alive with the obvious symbolic picture of the resurrection of the light of the World). There is something holy about the early morning hour, when Christ arose, and unholy about the darkness of night, the time when thieves are abroad and other kinds of unhealthy or unethical behaviour tend to take place. So, very probably, Benedict deliberately occupied his people with intervals of work and prayer from before daylight, with the pragmatic purpose of getting them good and tired, and tucked away, by the time the mischief of night begins.[20]

WHAT WILL HAPPEN IF WE DON'T OBSERVE DAILY PRAYER?

It seems that for most people, the reasons are twofold for why they don't observe daily prayer: (1) They never get around to it; and (2) The senses of their mind, soul and spirit become so full that focus upon God is squeezed out. An illustration of this was driven home to me in a recent trip to the Philippines. In Southeast Asia, while conducting a *Praying the Bible* seminar, the reality of our end-time culture really struck me. Outside the weather was sweltering and muggy. Workers seemed to drag themselves along the streets. The result was that people flocked to the malls like bees to a cool hive. There were thousands of youth and young adults just hanging out. The assault on their senses at the mall was unbelievable—pictures, music, images, television screens and computer games everywhere. No peace or solitude. Noise dominated the landscape. It's as though the mall were alive, and at a subconscious level, it was indoctrinating and creating a new culture—a new worldview.

I thought to myself, *What is this culture of Coca-Cola, McDonald's, Starbucks, MTV, Nickelodeon and the Internet?* It's all about you—what you will eat, what you will drink and how you can look beautiful. It's about the images, the sounds, the sell; it's all about man! The mall culture is not interested in leading its masses to think of God and then to stop and pray.

Of course, Coca-Cola or Starbucks is not bad in and of itself. And music and the Internet are only about entertainment . . . right? But where is God in all that? The answer is simple—He isn't! In the end, modern man is finding himself a million miles away from a God-centered life. Today, the whole world is becoming one gigantic mall, with one dominant language, culture and currency. But loving God with all of our heart, soul and strength, daily prayer and obeying the Ten Commandments are hardly to be found anywhere.

What the charismatic/evangelical church must realize is that it is the normal practice in Scripture that those who fear the Lord are to engage in audible, intentional, vocal praying of the Bible to God every day! The people of God of all ages have understood that loving and serving God requires the daily act of prayer. We should not minimize this vast testimony and experience. Like those who have gone out before us in faith, when we roll out of bed in the morning, we need to bless the Lord, and then again at noon we need to praise Him for his loving-kindness. Sometime throughout the day, we should actually stop and reaffirm our faith and devotion to God. Petition God and ask Him to change things. Then end each day with a focused, intentional and structured time of talking out loud to God. In other words, *"let us continually offer up a sacrifice of praise to God,* that is, the fruit of lips that give thanks to His name"* (Heb. 13:15, *NASB,* emphasis added).

Ultimately, if we don't respect the fact that this is a command of God, we will never seem to get around to it; we'll always be too busy. Not long ago, Stephen Covey became famous the world over for his *Seven Habits of Highly Effective People.* One of his seven habits was "first things first," or scheduling your time and life around what you truly believe and value. This was not just plain old time management, where lists and schedules allow you to do more. It was more the thinking through of what you truly believe are your values and then managing your life around them. Of course, most Christians would say that they truly value God and prayer. Yet the fact remains that they don't actually engage in focused, international prayer.

As we mentioned earlier, most of our time and money gets eaten up on pleasures of an undisciplined life. Whether we love it or hate it, television is a fixture in most American homes today. Apparently, 98 percent of households in the United States have at least one television set and 34 percent have two sets. According to the A. C. Nielsen Co., the average American watches 3 hours and 46 minutes of TV each day (that's more than 52 days of TV watching per year). By the age of 65, the average American will have spent nearly 9 years glued to the tube. In contrast to that, parents spend only 38.5 minutes per week in meaningful conversation with their children. Children of course are worse off in that they watch more TV than adults, but they are also spending extra time on the computer and digital games. The average child will see 30,000 TV commercials in a year.[21] Beyond sleeping and working, television watching is the single most time-consuming pastime of the Western culture.

From our point of view, we see how this can be used as useful leverage. Though our own children watch little or no TV (our TV hardly works and we refuse to buy cable), they love computer games and Internet chat lines with their friends. This is where we get the upper hand. In our house we say, "No pray, no play!" In our house, if the children want to enjoy the privileges of television or computer access with all its games and chat lines, then they need to be faithful with first things first. If that doesn't work, I half jokingly say, "No pray, no eat!" You've heard the old saying

WE MUST DISTINGUISH BETWEEN PRIVILEGE AND PUNISHMENT. IN OUR HOUSE WE SAY, "NO PRAY, NO PLAY!" IF THAT DOESN'T WORK, I HALF JOKINGLY SAY, "NO PRAY, NO EAT!"

Let's not let the tail wag the dog! Remember, television and videos, computer games, Nintendo and Internet chat lines are all privileges. Food also is a privilege, as at least half of the world's children go hungry. We tell our children, "If you cannot be faithful to love God, pray and be thankful, do you really believe you should be entitled to privileges?" We do not do our children any favors by letting them grow up disdaining the first commandment—to love the Lord their God—and growing dull of the call of God. If anyone thinks that this is legalism, then let's remember that Jesus Christ Himself did this, as did every family in His time. More accurately, we might say it was a cultural phenomena; that is, since one's peers and those around them did this, then it wasn't even a question of what was expected. For example, it is a given that the Muslims chant Koranic scriptures out loud to Allah five times a day. It's just something they do, no questions asked.

Perhaps the Christian community hasn't taken on a mentality of daily prayer because the majority of society does not do it. Daily prayer seems to be such a big deal when only a few are participating in it. Ask yourself this: What is the spiritual culture of your home? For our part, we decide to reject the lazy habits of society and choose to make a stand on daily prayer. What will you decide?

The same can be said to the adult population. Again, where does time go? If it is not pleasure, then work is the main pastime of the Western culture. Blessed with the richest lifestyle in the world, Western families still want more. More house, more space, more lawn, more toys! The only problem is that all this costs more money. More money means more time, energy and the application of life skills. The result is being too busy to pray.

Again, John Cassian, the leader of monks and a contemporary of Saint Augustine (c. A.D. 365 to 435) had a lot to say about this problem in his *Institutes*. Cassian was big on both corporate and private prayer. Writing to beginners in the monastic life, he applauds the Egyptian ideal of the monk. But he also observes the need for work to be coupled with prayer. If a monk prayed too many hours, he starved. But if he worked in the fields too long, he might as well be a farmer, not a monk. Cassian's balance lay in being aware of the danger of anxiety brought on by an inordinate amount of work that squeezed life out of our prayer life. He says:

> When a single coin would meet the necessities of our bodies we choose in our effort and in our work to earn two or even three. Similarly with a couple of tunics. It is sufficient to have one for the night and one for the day, but we try to have three or four.[22]

The main point is that life necessitates necessities, but this should not be a tension to the daily fixed hours of prayer and the life of the Spirit. But when the so-called necessities become only a cloak for covetousness and the busy man says, "I have no time to pray," then we most likely are busier than God intended us to be.

HOW DO WE APPLY DAILY PRAYER IN OUR LIVES?

To help you on your *pathway to spirituality,* begin to set aside a minimum of one, two or three focused times each day when you determine to pray the Bible out loud to God. Plan ahead of time when you are going to do this. For many of us, we have to become formal in managing our prayer time. In other words, we will need to use weekly planning calendars and commitments to friends in order to create a routine and eventually a habit of prayer. Mornings and evenings are good times for prayer, because it starts and finishes each day. A consistent time every day that becomes routine is preferable to mixing and matching. Yet ultimately the system that is chosen must be one that works for you. Always remember that the purpose for gathering is that His house will be a house of prayer. Do not let a single worship service go by without being totally engaged in it. Whether you gather with others or pray alone, the main thing is to make sure you are praying every day.

Of course, these focused times of prayer are not to be confused with the general constant communion that every child of God experiences on a continual basis. The goal is to stay in the Spirit all day long, communing quietly every moment of every day. It's important to talk back and forth, acknowledge the "small voice" and enjoy the presence of the Lord. Yet, regardless of how often these general stirrings come or how rare they are, make sure that they do not become a substitute for specific, focused daily times of prayer.

It's also important, especially in the beginning stages, to find someone who will hold you accountable so that you actually do show up for prayer regularly. The Jews and the monks and the nuns were all doing their daily prayers in the context of community (i.e., public, gathered, corporate worship). For them, private devotions and spontaneous prayers were icing on the cake. Therefore, we should not put all our eggs in the private prayer basket and we should put almost none in the public prayer basket. Praying Scripture out loud makes a great deal of sense in the presence of other people.

Mike Bickle says that when he first began to disciple himself in daily prayer, he started 18 prayer meetings a week—all with different people—just so that he would show up. Whether you pray with other people, go to a daily prayer meeting or operate on the buddy system, try and work with someone else who will spur you on as you spur them on.

Also, don't forget that the way to learn to pray is just to start. Practically speaking, everyone must start somewhere in time and space. Without planning this practical date with God, spiritual space is drowned out by the chatter of the world. This will not happen by itself. You are the only one who can make yourself show up. As mentioned earlier, even your children must be taught to show up. If the structure of daily prayer is neglected, then the foundation is missing. How does a teenager go to God and express his or her heart when he or she hasn't learned the discipline of prayer times? The prayer (word flow) is not there. The teenager has not been brought daily face-to-face with God. Soon, God fades away and he or she doesn't even know what to say to Him. On the contrary, if we would follow the example of Moses and Joshua, and cause our children to recite vocally out loud the Law to God daily, then our children would be in the habit of prayer and they would know what to say.

HOW LONG SHOULD WE PRAY?

One final question that might come to mind is this: How long should these set prayer times last? How long did people "show up" for daily prayer in the Bible? I asked a rabbi once how long it took for an Orthodox Jew to say his or her prayers. He said, "About 45 minutes to a hour." I said, "How long if you cheat?" "Oh," he said, "about 15 minutes."

Again, the original text of Scripture is quite revealing:

> Now Peter and John went up together into the temple at the hour of prayer, being the ninth hour (Acts 3:1, *KJV*).

Could it be that it was called the "hour of prayer" because it took approximately an hour to complete? We know that Benedict assigned at least two and a half hours of prayer a day, not counting the time assigned to holy reading.[23] In order to form the habit of daily prayer, we need to start teaching how to pray at a young age. A good starting place for children learning to pray is to engage them for 10 to 15 minutes and then work up to longer periods of time as they get older and as we, as teachers, mature more in our faith. It is especially important with children not to overdo it at the beginning. Make it interesting and desirable, or we'll run the risk of turning them off from God.

In summary, while there is no consensus as to the exact amount of prayer or time spent in prayer needed—whether it is two times daily (morning and evening), three times daily or even four times daily, which encompasses the three daily prayer times plus a night watch—what does hold true is that the righteous did pray every day and so fulfilled the injunction to pray *day and night.* Daily prayer causes our lives to be shaped not only around what we truly believe in and value, which is God, but also in that which God commands.

CHAPTER FOUR

PRAY TO GOD

This, then, is how you should pray: "Our Father in heaven, hallowed be your name, your kingdom come, your will be done on earth as it is in heaven. Give us today our daily bread. Forgive us our debts, as we also have forgiven our debtors. And lead us not into temptation, but deliver us from the evil one."

MATTHEW 6:9-13

When Jesus taught His disciples to pray, His very first point of teaching was to pray *to God*. By the way He told us to address God, He was teaching us that prayer is relationship with God the Father. Jesus addresses God in an intensely personal way. He calls Him *Abba,* which essentially means "Daddy." Prayer for Jesus is not the recitation of a wish list to some supreme cosmic force. Rather, it is communication with a Father who is interested in our daily lives here on Earth. He cares that we eat every day and that we get along with each other. He wants us to be free from temptation, and He wants us to be reminded that He has the power to keep us from evil. He wants us to pray for heaven on Earth because that is His desire for us. Obviously, Jesus knows Him intimately; and when He taught His disciples to pray, He wanted them to know God the same way He does—as Abba and Father. To know where to begin our prayer, we just need to pray *to God.*

In Jesus' day, as in our own, people believed in many gods. Even the concept of one supreme "sky-god" was not new. However, the God of the Bible differs from the typical supreme "sky-god" view in the following ways: (1) He has always existed and will always exist (see Rev. 21:6); (2) He creates out of nothing the things that are (see Heb. 11:3); and (3) He loves and listens to His chief creation—man. This third point is apparent throughout the Bible, but is particularly apparent in Jesus' address to God as Abba, Father. Jesus knew the One to whom He was praying.

Even though people everywhere pray, not everyone knows to whom they are praying. People do not pray the same way, nor do they pray with the same understanding of God. Some look within, some look without, some look to Earth and some look to the heavens. But since this is a book on Christian prayer, you may be thinking, *Of course I don't pray to any of those things—I pray to God. Who else is there?* However, this is not as self-evident as we might think.

Let's probe deeper. From the award-winning author Sophy Burnham, known for her best-seller *A Book of Angels,* we notice her popular panreligious view that sounds chic at first hearing but, upon close examination, contradicts itself. In her latest book, *The Path of Prayer,* she devoted an entire chapter to the question, What God do you pray to? She writes:

When, as a teenager, I abandoned my first images and definitions of God, I didn't know I was really asking how to pray. I thought the Great Question was "Who am I?" Or maybe "What's going on?" Neither did I know that it was utterly appropriate to leave behind my childhood images of God. Today I wonder what would have happened if that clergyman had merely listened to my confusion, my confession, and suggested, smiling, that my loss of faith was a blessing—was appropriate, ideal in fact, something to be applauded, not concerned about. What if he'd said that I lost faith not in God but in the God of my childish understanding, and that my very concept of God would change many times in my life, enlarge, widen, until finally it would involve no images at all?

Spirit, YHWH, Allah, Goddess (Kali, Mary, Lakshmi), Shiva, Buddha, Christ. How we pray, and when, reveals everything about what we think of God. Which is to say, what we think of the meaning of life. Is our vision optimistic, trusting, or is it dark and full of sin and guilt?

The fact is, God cannot be seen. He's like the wind. . . . The wind and the air are invisible to our weak eyes. It's the same with God, whose presence is glimpsed only in His works and seen only with the eyes of the heart.

Note I used the word "His" although I don't believe in a male deity. It is hard in Western culture to avoid the influence of the white-bearded grandfatherly pan-creator. In the East we come upon images of the fickle blue-skinned Krishna or of a variety of goddesses, from eight-armed deities dancing on one leg or to others with a thousand eyes. They are symbolic depictions, of course, as is Michelangelo's painting of God in the ceiling of the Sistine Chapel—the old man reaching out to touch and enliven the dormant Adam. It makes you understand why some faiths permit no images of God at all, lest they limit the limitless mystery.

Prayer presupposes a deity, but it need not be the masculine, tender, or suffering Christ, nor the guilt-inspiring Great White Judge in the Sky—nor, for that matter, any figure leaning down to listen to our pleas. People who have had an abusive or violent or alcoholic father visibly shudder at Jesus' metaphor of Our Father in Heaven—they'd rather have no God at all!—go atheist to save their sanity rather than submit to this vindictive prosecutor. (We want mercy, forgiveness—not judgment and justice!) I know people who refuse to cringe in guilt before the Holy One, aware only of how far they fail. Their life task is avoidance—to ensure that the beam of His attention falls on someone else.

The God of my understanding, meanwhile, evolved as I matured from being the pure spirit of my childhood to a figurative father or mother, to the mystery of both an impersonal and, simultaneously, intimately personal one. It is transcendence, immanent, eternal, unknowable. Yet, as a human, I also require a personal relationship, and I pray, therefore, to my Beloved, which is my husband, my sister, my mother, friend, and Lord. Sometimes I see it mediated through an angel. Sometimes it appears (a gasp of delight!) in a blooming flower. . . .

What, then, is our image? Are we approaching a tender mother? Attracting the attention of an absent-minded gift giver? Are we, like Saint Teresa, adoring the Christ, "His Majesty"? Or walking hand in hand with our best friend?

I know a nun who now laughs at her mistrustful Irish upbringing.

"If I wanted it," she explained, "God did not, and if God wanted it, it was going to involve hard sacrifice." If yours is the image of a punishing God, here's some advice: Divorce it! Choose one that's on your side. If God is in our minds, a projection of our highest being, then select a splendid deity.

I have a lot of trouble with the word "God." I like to use the words like "source," "force of the universe," or just "universe." Not only do I wish we had a better word for God but an ungendered one as well: not He, not She. But I am training myself to use the word "God," because it occurred to me recently that I'm the loser in the fight. I only know that there is something Out There and that it is also inside of me. It is both on my side and at my side. It is a part of me—and of you, and of that tree, that cat, the measureless waters of the ocean, the stars in an infinite night sky. The voice of the divine is singing in everything, and everywhere we look, if indeed we see with a loving heart, we see God flaming out. . . . God is pure essence. Beingness. It is YHWH: "I AM WHAT I AM" (as Moses learned at the Burning Bush). The Buddhists call it "suchness."[1]

It sounds so "nice," but is it true? Is God whoever we want Him to be or whatever works for us? Is God just one big bundle of love-essence, and it's only the religiously uptight people who have messed things up? Although this notion works well for politically correct, civic-sponsored lunches or prayer breakfasts in America, it doesn't work in the real world. The harsh reality is that the religions don't agree, and this turns out to be a very messy business. For instance, every hour, 18 Christians die a violent martyr's death somewhere in the world. Charles Colson states that "an average of one hundred and sixty thousand Christians have been killed every year since 1990 in places like Algeria, Nigeria, Sudan, and Pakistan."[2] That is over 400 Christian martyrs every day and over 200 million living in persecution—for no other crime than that they call Jesus Lord! The World Evangelical Alliance recently told the United Nations that "Christians are the largest single group in the world which is being denied human rights on the basis of their faith."[3] Sadly, the people who are doing the killing are mostly people of other religions and who are doing it because they believe "their" God says so! With all due respect, it's uninformed foolishness to say that we are all praying to the same God. After all, why is the same God telling half of His followers to kill the other half?

THE CLASH OF RELIGION

The present clash of civilizations poignantly illustrates the dilemma. Let's explore the religion of Islam to explain this. Muslims believe that there is no true god but Allah, and Muhammad is the messenger of Allah! Their insistence on monotheism is reminiscent of the God of the Bible. Although Islam does teach that Allah is the same God who was worshiped by Abraham, Isaac, Jacob, Moses, Ishmael and a host of other prophets, many Muslim scholars and mullahs believe that the testaments revered by Jews and Christians have no authority, as they believe they've been corrupted over the centuries. Thus, on every point where other religions differ from their religion, they assume that the records are wrong and that other presentations of God are forgeries. For people to maintain that there is no difference between Allah and Yahweh/God is to entirely dismiss the so-called revelations of the religion itself and superimpose upon it one's own belief as the authoritative view of all that is called God. On the other hand, Muslims do understand the difference, and evidently it matters to them enough to kill for it, which is condoned under the religious banner of *jihad*.

We must be honest and fair in saying that there are many peace-loving Muslims who abhor the violence that is presently being perpetrated by extremists and want to see it stop. What we are not talking about is the Muslim people as a whole, but rather what Islam teaches about itself. A distinction must be made between the belief and the people who believe it. People act out of what they believe; therefore, change the theology and you change behavior. So whether all Muslims practice it or not, what cannot be ignored is that the religion of Islam does teach and promote armed, violent submission to Islam. One of the main goals of Islam is the creation of a single Muslim nation with no geographical borders within it. As stated by Allah: "This, your community is a single community and I am your Lord; so worship Me."[4]

To accomplish this goal, whether in Israel or Indonesia, India or the Sudan, jihad is being declared on a near-daily basis. Religious jihad, as stated by the Muslims themselves, is sanctioned by Allah for the following reasons:

1. preserving the purity of Islam;
2. propagating Islam;
3. removing obstacles to Islam;
4. delivering man from those who enslave or restrict them;
5. stopping idol worship; and
6. making man submit to Allah.

Even though today there are two types of jihad, 75 percent of the references have to do with the violent expansion of Islam and the forced subjugation of the conquered. Only 25 percent of the references are of a symbolic nature—a kind of nonviolent internal struggle in order to become acceptable before Allah or metaphorically to join the struggle against injustice by helping the poor and needy. "The Jihad, as it became, turned into one of the mainstays of Muslim faith, having been conveyed to Muhammad, Muslims believe, directly from Allah through the Angel Gabriel. 'When you meet the unbelievers strike off their heads until you have massacred them,' says the Koran. 'Fight in the cause of Allah! . . . Kill them wherever you find them. Until they surrender. Then if they give over there shall be no enmity.'"[5]

To this end, Muhammad believed that Allah commanded the forced conversion of all Jews and Christians and, if they did not convert, armed subjugation and taxation was the penalty. The Koran says, "Jihad is ordained for you (Muslims) though you dislike it. Allah knows but you do not know" (*Surat-al-Baqarah* (2), *ayah* 216).

Most Western people do not realize that jihad is not new. From its inception and for 500 years thereafter, Islam established itself by the sword. From A.D. 632 until the time Europe responded with the Crusades, Muslim armies wiped out Christian communities from Morocco to Iraq. North Africa, Egypt and what is now present-day Turkey were the birthplaces of Christianity. They were Christian nations until the commencement of Islam with its violent jihad. The wars came because Islam taught—in the Koran—its faithful to "Fight against those who believe not in Allah nor in the Last Day, nor forbid that which has been forbidden by Allah and His Messenger [e.g., eating pork, drinking wine or people who say Jesus is Lord], and fight those who acknowledge not the Religion of Truth [i.e., Islam] from among the *People of the Book* [i.e., Christians and Jews] until they pay the jizya tax with willing submission, and feel themselves subdued" (*Surat-at-Tawbah* (9), *ayah* 29). Muhammad taught in the Koran

> The hour (of Judgment) will not begin until the Muslims fight the Jews and kill them. A Jew will hide behind a rock or a tree, and the rock or tree will say, "O Muslim, O slave of Allah! There is a Jew behind me, come and kill him!" (al-Bukhari 2926; Muslim 2921-2).[6]

While no one likes to see this, let alone believe it, this is the reality of millions of Christians living in the Islamic nations. Recently at the World Vision-sponsored International Prayer Consultation in South Africa, I talked to a man working in the poor Christian villages of Indonesia. The graphic pictures he had of men, women and children being beheaded, raped and mutilated by the jihad was beyond description. Indonesia boasts of being the largest Islamic nation, and from 1995 to this writing, religious jihads have burned and destroyed 1,000 churches, killed 5,000 Christians, seized or destroyed 100,000 shops and homes and produced 500,000 Christian refugees. All of this has occurred while the Indonesian government turned a blind eye, and the world hardly noticed. Since 1983, over 1 million Sudanese Christians have been slaughtered in their own country by government-sponsored jihad.

THE PURSUIT OF THE ONE TRUE GOD

The point is that what people believe about God does matter, and when people take it upon themselves to invent God in whatever image they perceive Him to be, some very bad theologies and practices emerge. Therefore, the first question should really be, How can we know anything about God in the first place? The question Which god is God? has been an innate curiosity of man from the beginning. Paul says in Romans 1 that all people intrinsically know that God exists through the evidence given in creation. This is the reason why people of every culture and of every age have sought to worship the One whom they instinctively know is greater than themselves. "He [God] has also set eternity in the hearts of men" (Eccles. 3:11). But without God's own revelations of Himself, man's attempt to figure Him out have been no more than extensions of his darkened mind. Moses was really the first prophet to "see" God and establish the authority of God beyond his own personal belief and culture. You might say that God established Himself first by revealing Himself to a people and then backing His authority up with signs and wonders.

A prime example is of God sovereignly revealing Himself when He appeared to Moses and telling him to go and represent "I AM that I AM" to Pharaoh:

> THE POINT IS THAT WHAT PEOPLE BELIEVE ABOUT GOD DOES MATTER, AND WHEN PEOPLE TAKE IT UPON THEMSELVES TO INVENT GOD IN WHATEVER IMAGE THEY PERCEIVE HIM TO BE, SOME VERY BAD THEOLOGIES AND PRACTICES EMERGE.

> So Moses and Aaron went to Pharaoh and did just as the LORD commanded. Aaron threw his staff down in front of Pharaoh and his officials, and it became a snake. Pharaoh then summoned wise men and sorcerers, and the Egyptian magicians also did the same things by their secret arts: Each one threw down his staff and it became a snake. But Aaron's staff swallowed up their staffs. Yet Pharaoh's heart became hard and he would not listen to them, just as the LORD had said (Exod. 7:10-13).

After Aaron's staff ate up the other staffs, the power struggle continued. Moses' staff turned the Nile to blood, but the Egyptian magicians did the same things by their secret arts (see Exod. 7:20-22). Then, Moses and Aaron stretched out their staffs over the waters and made the land teem with frogs, but the magicians of Egypt did the same through their secret arts:

> Then the LORD said to Moses, "Tell Aaron, 'Stretch out your staff and strike the dust of the ground,' and throughout the land of Egypt the dust will become gnats." They did this, and when Aaron stretched out his hand with the staff and struck the dust of the ground, gnats came upon men and animals. All the dust throughout the land of Egypt became gnats. But when the magicians tried to produce gnats by their secret arts, they could not. And the gnats were on men and animals. The magicians said to Pharaoh, "This is the finger of God." But Pharaoh's heart was hard and he would not listen, just as the LORD had said (Exod. 8:16-19).

The book of Exodus tells the story of how Yahweh eventually triumphed over Pharaoh and the other gods of Egypt. Pharaoh didn't have the choice of saying, "Well, that's just your interpretation of God, and we have our own gods. You get there your way, and we'll get there our way." No, 2 million Hebrew slaves historically got out of Egypt and became the recipients of the Law and the Ten Commandments, because God revealed Himself and backed it up with power. Ever since then, whether it's Joshua and the tumbling walls of Jericho, Elijah on Mount Carmel, Daniel in the lion's den or Jesus performing impossible signs and wonders, prophets have spoken what God said He wanted spoken, and then God backed it up with power.

The only reason any of us know anything at all about God is because of His initiative. The Word of God—that is, Jesus Christ—is the expression of God's perfect will. In creation, when God "spoke" the universe into existence, it was through the Word of God, who is the Son of God (see John 1:1-3,14). In any true revelation of God, the Word of God that is being communicated—whether recognized as the Son of God or not, whether a complete revelation or not—is Jesus Christ. None of us have any knowledge of God apart from Jesus.

When the Word became incarnate in Jesus Christ, God's perfect expression of His will became not just verbal or impersonal but visible, physical and intensely personal. And when the incarnate Word was crucified on the cross—in perfect obedience to the will of the Father—it was the ultimate expression and revelation of God's love for us. In other words, the one true, eternal, revealing God has existed from all eternity as God the Father, God the Son and God the Holy Spirit. The role of God's Holy Spirit is to bring truth home both through big splashy advertisements—like accomplishing signs and wonders—and through quieter things— like conversion to Jesus and changes of heart.

In the Bible, there are tried-and-true tests for determining whether so-called prophets are really speaking in God's name. First, their testimony must be consistent with what God has already revealed through the Word of God, Jesus Christ. Consider well these words from the mouth of Yahweh:

If a prophet, or one who foretells by dreams, appears among you and announces to you a miraculous sign or wonder, and if the sign or wonder of which he has spoken takes place, and he says, "Let us follow other gods" (gods you have not known) "and let us worship them," you must not listen to the words of that prophet or dreamer. The LORD your God is testing you to find out whether you love him with all your heart and with all your soul. It is the LORD your God you must follow, and him you must revere. Keep his commands and obey him; serve him and hold fast to him. That prophet or dreamer must be put to death, because he preached rebellion against the LORD your God, who brought you out of Egypt and redeemed you from the land of slavery; he has tried to turn you from the way the LORD your God commanded you to follow. You must purge the evil from among you (Deut. 13:1-5).

Signs and wonders can deceive as well as enlighten; they can be false as well as true. Pharaoh's magicians had some pretty cool effects in their bags of tricks, but they could have been relying on demons for their power. False prophets with power are also predicted in the New Testament. Jesus said the signs and wonders of false prophets can deceive even the elect (see Matt. 24:24; Mark 13:22). Paul also expected false prophets to accomplish signs and wonders (see 2 Thess. 2:9). It is clear from these passages that if any so-called prophet receives revelation that leads toward other gods, we are not to believe them, even if they say, "We worship the same God."

The second test is that God backs up His message with spiritual power. This is what happened in the New Testament Church (see Acts 2:19,22,43; 4:30; 5:12; 14:3; Rom. 15:19; 2 Cor. 12:12;

Heb. 2:4) and was Paul's expectation of how God would work through the proclamation of the gospel:

> And I, brethren, when I came to you, came not with excellency of speech or of wisdom, declaring unto you the testimony of God. For I determined not to know any thing among you, save Jesus Christ, and him crucified. And I was with you in weakness, and in fear, and in much trembling. And my speech and my preaching was not with enticing words of man's wisdom, but in demonstration of the Spirit and of power: that your faith should not stand in the wisdom of men, but in the power of God (1 Cor. 2:1-5, *KJV*).

The third test is character. In the Bible, one's behavior in life is of utmost importance. Prophets of God are not expected to be perfect, but they are supposed to exhibit the kind of life that commends people to God, rather than one that repels them from God. The apostle John wrote these words:

> Dear children, do not let anyone lead you astray. He who does what is right is righteous, just as he is righteous. He who does what is sinful is of the devil, because the devil has been sinning from the beginning. The reason the Son of God appeared was to destroy the devil's work. Dear children, let us not love with words or tongue but with actions and in truth (1 John 3:7-8,18).

In the Bible, living the truth and loving through actions are nonnegotiable. If these things are important for ordinary believers, then for prophets—who are claiming to speak messages from God—they are that much more important!

Thus, the only reason we know anything concrete about God at all is because He has invaded history and disclosed Himself to us. The way we know that those who speak in His name are true is because of their doctrine (teaching), power and character. Their revelation must align with previous revelation. Therefore, although Muhammad truly felt he believed in the God of Abraham, Isaac and Ishmael, and though he might've meant well with his reform, the extra biblical "revelation" he received was not consistent with the revelation of Moses, the prophets and Jesus. He did not experience God backing the revelation up with signs and wonders, and the fruit or character that flowed from its teaching was not the same fruit that the Bible requires. Today, there is no other religion older than the God of Abraham, Isaac and Jacob, and no deity, whether from Egypt, India, China or Babylon, that is older than the recorded self-revelation of Yahweh.

THE CONNECTION BETWEEN GOD AND MAN

What do you see when you close your eyes to pray? If 100 people were to try and draw a picture or write a description of what they see when they close their eyes today, we would be surprised to find that we would have as many different visions as we have people. Ultimately, we are still bound to the fundamental principle that God is who God says He is, not who we think He is. We are made in His image, not the other way around. Just as other religions may have perceptions of God that are not true, even so-called Christians may be praying to a false notion of God. Do we want to be praying to an extension of our own imagination? Consider the differences of perspectives as to who God is even amongst those who call themselves Christians. Do the people of each sect really pray to a true representation of the Yahweh of the Bible? For instance, to whom do Mormons pray? To whom do Jehovah's Witnesses pray? To whom do most contemporary charismatic evangelical believers pray? In the end, we come back to the fundamental question, Who is God? Is God some big Santa Claus in heaven whose main purpose is to give out gifts and get us out of trouble now and again?

> GOD IS WHO GOD SAYS HE IS, NOT WHO WE THINK HE IS. WE ARE MADE IN HIS IMAGE, NOT THE OTHER WAY AROUND.

KNOW GOD THROUGH HIS SELF-REVELATION

We can only truly know God through His self-revelation. For this reason, I have found it extremely helpful to pray the revelations or visions of God. Often, when speaking on the topic of prayer, I ask a congregation to stand up so that I can give them a test. The statement I give to them is this: If you know the location of at least four of the many God sightings in the Bible, and you can generally recount what the prophet saw, then stay standing. At first, people begin to look around dumbfounded. Then, slowly, with sheepish sideways glances, almost everyone begins to sit down. Rarely is there even one to three percent of the audience left standing. Not many people are in the regular practice of praying the theophanies—that is, the "God sight-ings." They are not even familiar with the concept.

After giving the test, I go further. I ask an engaged couple to stand up. Giggling nervously, at least one couple always com-plies. I put up a large paper barrier between them and begin to paint an imaginary scenario based on Genesis 24. What if I were Eliezer, the servant of Abraham, out looking for a wife for Isaac. Suddenly, I come upon you. You are beautiful and have fulfilled the signs I asked for (i.e., willing to draw water for all of my camels and so on). Then I ask if you would like to come back with me to meet your husband. I ask the obvious question, "Would you like to see your husband?" Every young fiancée nods eagerly. I ask, "Why would you like to see a picture of him?" They always want to see what he looks like; they always want to know what they are getting. Then I apologize, saying that photographs aren't invented yet, but I do have a very detailed description of what someone who saw him says he looks like. "Would you like the description?" I ask. "Oh, for sure I would like it; I want to at least read about what he looks like," responds the fiancée.

Turning to the man, I go through the same scenario. "Would you like to see a picture?" I ask. "Yeah, sure." "Well, sorry, there isn't one. How about a detailed description?" "Yes, I want it." The point of this illustration is that there is hardly any couple on Earth—given the reality that photographs don't exist—who would not want at the very least a detailed account of the one they are betrothed to. Why is it, then, that almost all people who say they love God and who are espoused to His Son as the Bride of Christ are unaware of the "visions of God" in the Bible—the theophanies—and are unable to recount them?

The word "theophanies" derives its meaning from two Greek words: *theos* and *phaino*. "Theos" means "God" and "phaino" means "to appear or show"; hence, the "God appearances." The details of these God sightings reveal to us visions of the anthropomorphism of God, and to some extent, His actions. They describe, at different times, where He lives, who is around Him, the color of His hair and eyes, what He is wearing, the many sounds of His voice and so on. If we want to know God better, we should start by talking to God as He revealed Himself to be. When we pray the passages in the Bible that reveal God in physical form, abstract attributes become embodied by a very personal God. God becomes not just remote and far off but close and personal. Every word of the descriptions of the "visions of God" reveal more about who God is and the nature of His Person (see chapter 7). With other theophanies, you will familiarize yourself with the sights, sounds and smells of heaven—you will "see" who you are talking to.

> THE THEOPHANIES ARE THE "GOD APPEARANCES"—THE "VISIONS OF GOD."

In an effort to learn to pray to God several years ago, I began to pray a prayer based on Revelation 4:2-11 (*NASB*):

Immediately I was in the Spirit; and behold, a throne set in heaven, and One sat on the throne. And He who sat there was like a jasper and a sardius stone in appearance; and there was a rainbow around the throne, in appearance like an emerald. Around the throne were twenty-four thrones, and on the thrones I saw twenty-four elders sitting, clothed in white robes; and they had crowns of gold on their heads. And from the throne proceeded lightnings, thunderings and voices. And there were seven lamps of fire burning before the throne, which are the seven spirits of God. Before the throne there was a sea of glass, like crystal. And in the midst of the throne, and around the throne, were four living creatures full of eyes in front and in back. The first living creature was like a lion, the second living creature like a calf, the third living creature had a face like a man, and the fourth living creature was like a flying eagle. And the four living creatures, each having six wings, were full of eyes around and within. And they do not rest day or night, saying:

"Holy, holy, holy, Lord God Almighty, who was and is and is to come!"

Whenever the living creatures give glory and honor and thanks to Him who sits on the throne, who lives forever and ever, the twenty-four elders fall down before Him who sits on the throne and worship Him who lives forever and ever, and cast their crowns before the throne, saying:

"You are worthy, O Lord, to receive glory and honor and power;

For You created all things,

And by Your will they exist and were created."

I also went into Revelation 5 and read the description of "thousands upon thousands, and ten thousand times ten thousand" of angels around the Lamb of God (v. 11). These passages are alive with unbelievably intense movement, color and sound.

This is heaven, God's dwelling place, and as I prayed these passages, I began to understand more about Him. I discovered that as I gazed at just His surroundings, a lot about the way I thought about the nature of God changed. I repeatedly prayed the "God passages" (see Isa. 6; Ezek. 1–3; Dan. 7; Rev. 1; 4) until I knew them intuitively. As I did this, I truly began—for perhaps the first time in my life—to pray *to God*. I went to His throne room in my spirit. I placed myself before Him in His surroundings. Doing so allowed me to see more clearly what He could do when I invoked Him to come to my surroundings. Faith grew in me as I saw Him for who He is. The authority of the universe rests in Him. Every angelic being falls repeatedly at His feet. Thousands upon thousands attend Him. He is the Lamb in the center of the throne. He is the Ancient of Days, seated on a throne of fire. He is awesome to behold. Majesty and honor surround Him; everyone around Him adores Him with shouts of worthy and holy and glorious praise.

PRAY THE SCRIPTURES OUT LOUD TO GOD

When teaching on prayer, I constantly say, "If you want to 'see' God, pray Revelation 4 out loud to God 100 times, and then you will 'see' God." If anyone were to pray Revelation 4 five times through a day for 20 days, there

> IF YOU WANT TO "SEE" GOD, PRAY REVELATION 4 OUT LOUD TO GOD 100 TIMES, AND THEN YOU WILL "SEE" GOD.

is no question that they would be able to close their eyes and instantly picture heaven.[7] Having access in our minds to the words and images of the heavenly throne room is crucial to God becoming personal to us. We should be able to "see" God and become as familiar with heaven as we are with our own homes. Since our youngest daughter was four years old, we taught her to pray all the way through Revelation 4. At night we can say, "Vashti, close your eyes and tell us what you see in heaven?" In a second, she will begin to walk through the entire heavenly vision. For her, the abstract has become personal.

FOCUS YOUR ATTENTION ON WHOM YOU ARE PRAYING TO

Some may question at this point if God really looks like the visions as seen by the prophets. Amazingly, the prophets, spanning centuries of time, are consistent with one another in what they saw. Whether it is Moses, Daniel, Isaiah, Ezekiel or John, they all saw much the same thing. Although it is true that God is a Spirit (see John 4:24), when He reveals Himself to humankind, He embodies form and substance: There was a throne with someone sitting on it (see Rev. 4:2). Moses says that when he "entered the Tent of Meeting to speak with the LORD, he heard the voice speaking to him from between the two cherubim above the atonement cover on the ark of the Testimony. And he [God] spoke with him" (Num. 7:89). That is, in the Tabernacle, the voice of God was located "here" as opposed to "there." Although God's presence is everywhere, He can also be present in particular times and places. God is able to break through infinitely in order to manifest His presence in concrete ways. God wants to be seen not just as a general "everywhere" presence in the universe but as a God who is personal and reveals Himself as He gets involved with us.

Moreover, Jesus also becomes a focal point of prayer for the same reasons. The incarnation of Jesus is the supreme example of God revealing Himself to mankind. Jesus, the Word of God, became flesh and dwelt among us (see John 1:14). Jesus said, "Anyone who has seen me has seen the Father" (John 14:9). Common practice of the saints throughout history has been to focus upon the person and works of Jesus:

> Teresian prayer is characteristically Christ centered. Christ is the direct object of both the mental and the affective dynamics of Teresian prayer. Teresa prays with, to, and through Jesus Christ. Her Christ is the Christ of the Gospels; Christ as the "Way, the Truth, and the Life" is her constant focus. That focus must be learned by the beginner, retained by those advanced in prayer, and refined into a "loving gaze" by the contemplative. Some of her principles in this area are that:
>
> · Meditation's best subject and object is the biblical Christ in His life, death, and resurrection;
>
> · One's prayer is best habitually (though not exclusively) centered on Christ; and
>
> · The sacred humanity of Christ is the most adequate meditation for initial growth in prayer and the best assurance of and preparation for the gift of contemplation.[8]

FINAL THOUGHTS

In conclusion, we are calling people to pray *to God*. Focusing attention on who we are praying *to* is central to prayer. The prayer of faith is largely dependent on what we believe about

God and His ability and desire to answer prayer. As stated earlier, Joshua was commanded to meditate on the Law. As we meditate specifically on the passages that delineate God's vision and attributes, a major shift will happen in our prayer lives. We will have more faith. We will see that our God truly is an awesome God. We will see—as David did—His beauty. We will increase in the fear of the Lord. Our intercession will be less problem oriented and more solution oriented, because we will see Him—His vastness and His tenderness, His power and His concern—over and about all that we deal with on Earth. With other theophanies, we will familiarize ourselves with the sights, sounds and smells of heaven; we will "see" who we are talking to. We will have confidence that God is the One who has all power in heaven and Earth to answer. Search the Scriptures for every description you can find of Him—from the prophets to the Gospels, from Mount Sinai to the Cross, to heaven and back—and then start all of your intercession, petition and devotion by praying *to God*.

CHAPTER FIVE

PRAY THE BIBLE

Learning to pray the Bible is like courtship. At first, because the two people involved don't know each other well, there is the awkward phase of not knowing what to say. They have chosen to see each other exclusively and have set the time and place for the big date. However, now that the date has arrived, what are they going to say to each other?

The courtship with God through prayer is even more difficult, as the Person we are talking to is wholly other than us. His ways are higher than ours. His thoughts are higher than ours as well. Therefore, in talking *to God,* how can we figure out what to say for those long periods of silence? What does He like to talk about? Before we learned to pray—after setting our hearts and schedules, and getting everything in order to seek His face—we found we had virtually no vocabulary with which to speak to Him. Let's illustrate this.

Wesley went to Nigeria, Africa, when he was about 21 years old. He lived in the bush and didn't speak Nigerian. Nigeria, however, has a language rich in greetings. He found that if he learned at least 25 different greetings, he could carry on minimal conversation with greetings alone. Because he so flamboyantly greeted everyone who came by, the locals thought he spoke the language fluently. They would immediately engage him in conversation, speaking rapidly, expecting him to understand what was being said. While on the outside he was smiling and nodding, on the inside he was drawing blanks.

While he was in Africa, he would occasionally go visit a little old lady named Mama Ola. This is how he describes his visits with her:

At times I had an interpreter, but often I went alone. Before we led her to Christ, she was banished from the village under suspicion of being a witch just because her young daughter died. She was crippled and deformed—an outcast of society. Since she had no friends whatsoever, I tried to visit her as often as I could. Our meetings went something like this: Coming down the track, I would begin to shout greetings from afar. She in return would hear and begin to greet me back. As I got closer, there would be bows, smiles and greetings for a nice day. If we hadn't seen each other for a longer period of time, we would bow again and go on for another five minutes, doing this and that back and forth.

Finally, with greetings finished, I would enter her little mud-brick hut. As a sign of respect, she would sit me on the better of the two wooden stools and sweep away some dirt from the already dirt floor. Sitting down across from me, she would give a few more winding-down greetings, saying in essence that she was really glad to see me again. Soon, however, silence would reign and I would begin to look around the hut.

Spider webs rested in every corner and smoke filled the top of the hut from the cooking fire. A few beams of sunlight poked through the mud-brick wall. A cock-roach, ant or some other crawly thing would move around on the ground until I stepped on it. Then Mama Ola would fuss with some weathered old rags. She would pull out her prized kola nut, break me off a piece and we would both crunch happily. Then she'd say loudly in Nigerian, "My bananas are growing well, aren't they?" hoping that the increase in volume would make up for the lack of understanding. Politely, I looked outside and responded, "Yes, it is a nice day outside, Mama." Obviously, we didn't have a clue what the other was say-ing. After a moment more of silence, Mama would tweak my cheek and laugh conversationally. I would respond in kind by saying, "Yes, Mama," and then pat her on the knee. I would give her a few basic supplies and she would thank me profusely. She too liked to give, so she would offer me a boiled egg. Once the gifts were exchanged, we would just look around again, doing nothing but sitting in each other's presence. After about 10 minutes, I'd begin to say, "Well, I'd better go, Mama," and this would initiate the entire greetings ritual all over again. There was a minimum of 10 different good-bye and thank-you-for-coming tribal greetings. The feelings were heartfelt and the appreciation real. Yet despite all the sense of presence, we never were able to delve deeper into our feelings, thoughts and so on. Due to the language barrier, our real knowledge of one another was handicapped.

DIFFERENT LANGUAGES AND INTERPRETATION STYLES CAN CAUSE COMMUNICATION BARRIERS

This illustration aptly describes the prayer lives of most people. We have a great number of clichés, a lot of greetings and a variety of wonderful adjectives. However, when all is said and done, we haven't said much of anything with depth or meaning. Therefore, we usually run out of words and stop praying out loud—doing it in our heads instead. Then, unfortunately, our minds begin to wander, and soon we are not praying at all.

This may be particularly true of men. Most men do well in groups—marching around and talking and praying on surface issues—but when the time comes to say something of substance, they are speechless. Most men prefer action. They are good at building and counting, shifting this, constructing that, putting up walls and moving piles of dirt. But when the action stops, men have a tendency either to fall asleep or start thinking of new ways to build and count. On the other hand, most women, who by nature are more nurturing and relational, often find conversation and, consequently, prayer, easier to do. They want to talk. When a husband comes home from work and is silent, a wife will often complain, "Why don't you talk to me?" This is a question men have difficulty answering, because they don't understand what she's asking.

Therefore, he usually responds, "I did. I just talked to you now. I said 'Hello.'"

"No, no," she says, "I want you to *talk* to me." In an effort to comply, the man will spout off on what he has built, how many piles he moved and how much money he made. But the wife wants more. "No, no, talk to me about what's inside."

"What's inside?" seems like a strange question to a guy who has no idea that she wants to interact about feelings. So for most opposite-sex relationships, communication breaks down.

Many women naturally have this empathetic understanding of a deeper conversational life, which leads to deeper relationships. However, most men need to be taught to talk like this. In fact, there are expensive weeklong seminars on teaching men how to talk to their wives, but unfortunately, there aren't too many on teaching men how to talk to God. A wife is only the first frontier, but God is the final frontier. It's one thing to learn the vocabulary of feeling words necessary for talking to wives; it is quite another to learn the vocabulary of spiritual words necessary for communion with God, who is Spirit. "God is spirit, and his worshipers must worship in spirit and in truth" (John 4:24).

LEARN TO COMMUNICATE

Male and female differences have the potential to emerge in language learning. For example, when a guy doesn't know what to say, he will usually just start *doing* something. Psychologists tell

us that girls are more verbal, but for guys, talking is more difficult because they can't see immediate results. Talking to someone—whether to a person of the opposite sex or to God—is
usually more difficult for men. Therefore, most men, if they
pray, pray at night just as they are going to bed. "Oh, God, thank
you for the day. And God, bless . . . ZZZzzz." This is the basic
North American male's prayer life. He doesn't know what to say.
He needs words because he doesn't have his own words.

Additionally, because men usually must have words set before
them to pray and communicate, they usually connect better with
God during worship rather than in the prayer room. Church worship can be very meaningful to a guy. He comes into a building
where he is made to stand up so he doesn't fall asleep. There is a
worship leader—the equivalent of a coach—who can carry a tune,
because he can't. Somebody has written down the words for him,
and they are printed out for all to see. There is enough noise to
drown out his croaky voice, which he's afraid of. The whole structure facilitates talking to God even though it's through singing.
After about 10 minutes, he thinks, *Hmmm, I kind of like this. It feels
good.* But when he goes home, he's scared of his own voice, he
doesn't have the tune, he can't remember the words and he is
stuck again. At that point he's back to mental prayer, which then
instigates the wandering mind . . . the ball game . . . the beach.

THE BIBLE RELEASES POWER IN PRAYER

How do we talk to God? Initially as I listened to Mike Bickle's
series on prayer, *The Life of the Warrior,* the most revolutionary
thing I heard was, "Pray to God using the prayers of the Bible."
This was perplexing. How can I pray to God by praying someone

else's prayers? Pray Bible prayers? Am I sure I heard that right? I seriously doubted the efficacy of such an approach, but my own prayers were so boring that I felt I had nothing to lose in trying Bickle's way. To my surprise, it turned out to be the beginning of a major transformation in my prayer life. The Bible is actually a whole book of spiritual words! The Bible will teach you the language of God so that you can effectively communicate to Him. When you speak from the Bible in your prayers, you will be led to an entirely different place in prayer—one you might've not thought was humanly possible—simply because the language of the Bible is so absolutely different from our own. In fact, at times you're not even going to understand what you're saying because of this vast difference. You will, however, learn a new language—the language of the Spirit. It's what we call God-talk.

> BECAUSE WE DON'T KNOW WHAT TO SAY, GOD GAVE US THE WORDS TO PRAY THE BIBLE!

As with any language, the language of prayer needs to be learned. By profession, Stacey is a high school French and German teacher. She knows what it is like to teach beginners a new language; it is not easy. Even the most motivated students stumble and fall in trying to express themselves in a foreign language. Biblical language is, in many ways, a foreign language. First Corinthians 2:13 says:

> This is what we *speak*, not in *words* taught us by human wisdom but in *words* taught by the Spirit, expressing *spiritual truths* in *spiritual words* (emphasis added).

The Bible contains spiritual words, which, according to this verse, are different from our ordinary, human words. Therefore, like a new student, we need to go through the sometimes painful process of learning the language of the Spirit so that we will be better able to express our hearts to God and learn His heart for us.

Although the idea of praying the Bible is neither new nor novel, it certainly was a radical concept to me. I was shocked to discover that for thousands of years, men and women of God had used the model of praying the Bible—out loud—to God—every day (see Josh. 1:8; Eph. 5:18-20; Col. 3:16)! How can we express what a gross oversight it is that we have spent many years in Bible colleges and seminaries but did not even know that the bulk of Christians have always prayed the Bible—a practice known for centuries as the *lectio divina,* or the divine reading. As mentioned earlier, we began to realize that we were not doing prayer right, because our modern methods discounted thousands of years of tradition and, at the same time, did not offer a better replacement. In most cases, modern Western Christians love God and think about Him often, yet they actually pray less than 15 minutes a day.

From the beginning, God told Joshua to meditate on the Book of the Law "day and night" (Josh. 1:8). Of course, the Law contained the very words of God spoken directly to Moses. In other words, the *logos,* or Word of God at the beginning of the Bible, was the Mosaic Law. The description given by Moses is

> The LORD called to Moses and *spoke to him from the Tent of Meeting.* He said, "Speak to the Israelites and say to them . . . " (Lev. 1:1-2, emphasis added).

Everyone in Israel was in awe when Moses would go to hear God speak to him directly:

> As Moses went into the tent, the pillar of cloud would come down and stay at the entrance, while the LORD spoke with Moses. Whenever the people saw the pillar of cloud standing at the entrance to the tent, they all stood and worshiped, each at the entrance to his tent. The LORD would speak to Moses face to face, as a man speaks with his friend (Exod. 33:9-11).

Moses, the friend of God, would listen as God spoke to him. He then taught the words of God to Joshua and the rest of the Israelites. They, in turn, taught it to their children and so on. Most of us don't realize that every Jewish boy was expected to have memorized the entire Torah, or first five books of Moses, by the time they were bar mitzvahed at 13 years old.[1] They would chant (pray) the words of God every day of their lives.

THE PEOPLE OF GOD HAVE ALWAYS PRAYED THE BIBLE.

DAVID'S PERSISTENT PRAYER LIFE

In fact, the people of God have always prayed the Bible. From Moses to Joshua to David to Jesus and beyond, the command of meditating on God's Law was obeyed. Over 400 years after Moses and Joshua, during the time of David, you still find the Israelites keeping the command of praying the Law every day. The testimony of David was that he delighted in the Law of the LORD, and on his Law he meditated "day and night" (Ps. 1:2).

The result of David's delight and of his time sitting in front of the ark, following Moses' example, is many of the psalms. David wasn't kidding when he said he delighted in God's Law. He wrote Psalm 119—the longest chapter in the Bible—containing 176 verses, all on the benefits of meditating on the Law. It is an alphabetical acrostic on the glories of God's Word. It is so glorious that Campbell McAlpine has made a list of 54 benefits of meditating on the Word from this psalm alone.[2] Love for the Word of God and worship are natural responses that proceed from praying the Bible:

> I will worship toward Your holy temple, and praise Your name for Your lovingkindness and Your truth; for *You have magnified Your word above all Your name* (Ps. 138:2, *NKJV*, emphasis added).

David clearly understood the importance of praying the Word of God. So did John. When Jesus manifested Himself in the flesh, John stated that He was the fulfillment of the Law:

> The Word became flesh and made his dwelling among us (John 1:14).

> Do not think that I have come to abolish the Law or the Prophets; I have not come to abolish them but to fulfill them (Matt. 5:17).

David spent so much time in daily meditation on the Law—he was so immersed in it and, consequently, so passionate about the glory of God—that God's Spirit inspired him to write many of the psalms and create a new worship genre—the worship of the heart. Catalyzed by David, the Psalms subsequently became the prayer book for all of Israel and later on for the Early Church as well. It is also evident that Solomon, David's son, knew the Psalms and the Law of Moses intimately. The chroniclers record how Solomon knew from both his father and the reading of the Law how to build the

> DAVID PRAYED THE BIBLE AND WE GOT THE PSALMS.

Temple and situate the ark in the holy place (see 2 Chron. 5). In his dedication prayer in 2 Chronicles 6, he quotes directly and indirectly the Psalms and the Law frequently (see Deut. 12:11; Pss. 33:18; 34:15; 89:24,28; 132:8-9).

JONAH'S ROAD TO PRAYING THE BIBLE

Jonah is the same. Two hundred and fifty years after David, his prayer from the belly of the great fish is full of psalms, as you can see from the chart below:

Jonah 2:2	Psalms 18:5-6; 86:13; 88:1-7
Jonah 2:3	Psalm 42:7
Jonah 2:4	Psalm 5:7
Jonah 2:6	Psalms 18:5; 116:3
Jonah 2:7	Psalms 18:6; 77:10-11; 142:3
Jonah 2:9	Psalms 3:8; 50:14,23

What would Jonah have done if he hadn't known the Psalms? Had he not been in the practice of praying the Psalms, perhaps he never would have gotten out of the belly of that whale!

DANIEL'S PATH TO SUCCESSFUL PRAYER

As we go on in time, we continue to see the people in the Bible praying the Bible. The prayer life of the prophet Daniel shows that he was also in the practice of meditating on the Law of God. His famous prayer of intercessory repentance in Daniel 9:4 begins with a quote from Deuteronomy 7:9:

> "Alas, O Lord, the great and awesome God, who keeps His covenant and lovingkindness for those who love Him and keep His commandments" (*NASB*).

The corollary passage in Deuteronomy 7:9 reads: "He is God, the faithful God, who keeps His covenant and lovingkindness to a thousandth generation with those who love Him and keep His commandments" (*NASB*).

Daniel's understanding of the character of God is formed from the Law. Therefore, he has great boldness in approaching God on the basis of the Covenant God made with His people. As Daniel continues in prayer, we see in Deuteronomy 7:10-11 that his understanding of what has happened in Israelite history is based on Deuteronomy 27:15-26. Because the Israelites disobeyed God's teachings—which they clearly knew—they were responsible for the curses that the Law said would fall on the disobedient. Daniel's prayer is not filled with excuses; rather, he acknowledges that the Israelites clearly knew the Law and were deliberately disobedient.

> We have not obeyed His voice. . . . We have sinned, we have been wicked. . . . We are not presenting our supplications before Thee on account of any merits of our

own, but on account of Thy great compassion (Dan. 9:14,15,18, *NASB*).

Basically, Daniel put his hope in the character of God, which He also would have known from the Law (see Exod. 34:6-7.) The whole of his prayer is praying back to God what He already revealed about who He was and what He would do.

OTHER PROPHETS' PRAYERS TO GOD

The important thing to note is that we see from the prayers of the later prophets that their prayers were largely based on praying the sections of the Bible that they had in their times. Habakkuk prays in Habakkuk 3:2:

LORD, I have heard of your fame; I stand in awe of your deeds, O LORD.

In Jehoshaphat's famous prayer, when he faced annihilation from surrounding enemies, we discover that his appeal to God is based on God's covenant with Abraham (see 2 Chron. 20:6-12). Jehoshaphat calls to God because the enemies that are after him are in violation of God's promises to his friend Abraham.

By the time you get to the New Testament, we find Jesus and the apostles praying in the Temple at the set times of prayer (see chapter 3). Jesus makes several direct quotes from the Old Testament, and even the traditional Lord's Prayer was made up of snippets of Old Testament phrases and theology (see Exod. 20:7; 1 Chron. 17:11; 29:11; Pss. 25:18; 95:8; 140:1; Prov. 30:8; Jer. 3:9). Indeed, virtually all of the Eighteen Benedictions prayed daily by every Jew were nothing more than a paraphrase and composite of Old Testament Law and theology (see appendix C). Paul was "educated under Gamaliel, strictly according to the law of our fathers" (Acts 22:3, *NASB*). As a strict Pharisee, Paul would have been used to chanting the entire Torah (Book of the Law), all the Psalms and great chunks of the prophets (if not the whole of the prophets). Without a doubt, both Jesus and Paul learned the Law and continued to pray the Law through the prevalent Jewish practice of chanting it out loud (meditating on it) daily.

PRAYER HAS BEEN PASSED DOWN FOR OUR BENEFIT

Hundreds of years later, the monks and nuns of Europe were still carrying on the age-old practice of praying Scripture. Their prayer book was the Psalms. Saint Patrick (c. A.D. 389-461) testified that as a teenager, he was kidnapped by fierce Celtic barbarians and sold into slavery in Ireland, where he was forced to herd swine and sheep. He began to despair of his very life. Up to this point, he had rejected the Christian faith of his childhood; but then slowly, in the cold, damp hills of Ireland, the Lord began to make Patrick aware of his unbelief and rebellion. Slowly he began to call out to the God of his father. He writes:

> When I came to Ireland I tended herds every day and I used to pray many times during the day. More and more my love of God and reverence for him began to increase. My faith grew stronger and my zeal so intense that in the course of a single day I would say as many as a hundred prayers, and almost as many in the night. This I did

even when I was in the woods and on the mountains. Even in times of snow or frost or rain I would rise before dawn to pray. I never felt the worse for it; nor was I in any way lazy because, as I now realize, I was full of enthusiasm.[3]

The prayers that Patrick mentions were written prayers learned as a child—most likely the Psalms. The foundation of Patrick's prayer life became the cornerstone of Celtic spirituality.

If you examine the history of praying the Bible, you will find that it was common practice for all monks and nuns to pray the Psalms by reciting them together daily. In fact, in the *Rule of Saint Benedict* (c. A.D. 480-547), it is

> THE MONKS AND NUNS OF EUROPE ORDERED THE PRIVATE RECITAL DAILY OF THE "THREE FIFTIES," THAT IS, THE WHOLE PSALTER EVERY DAY.

prescribed that the entire Psalter of 150 Psalms should be recited during the week. Columban, however, ordered that during the winter months, for instance, 330 psalms were to be covered weekly at Matins alone and some 250 at other canonical hours of prayer. St. Columban pointed out that he was following the tradition of his countrymen who delighted in the psalms.[4]

In other words, with more time in the winter months, the community would spend more time together praying the Psalms.

As the practice of praying the Bible spread, the Irish monks of the sixth and seventh centuries took it to a point of obsession:

> Psalmody was held in great honour, as the essential part of the cursus of the liturgy. Practically all knew the Psalms by heart; Latin had been a foreign tongue to them and the Psalter was their primer. The Psalms were explained by means of glosses in Celtic; . . . as soon as they understood them, they learnt them by heart. . . . Many Rules even ordered the private recital daily of the "three fifties," that is, the whole Psalter everyday.[5]

This is amazing. Not only did the medieval Church pray together on a daily basis, but many followers prayed the entire book of Psalms daily. Imagine what happened when they got to Psalm 119, the longest chapter in the Bible. The medieval Church was a praying Church, and they learned the language of prayer by praying the Bible:

> Pondering sacred Scripture was the way the early monks, the desert fathers and mothers, and in fact the people of the Bible, prayed. And the monks developed a traditional method for doing that, the ingredients of which we find rehearsed in John of the Cross when he writes: "Seek in *reading* and you will find in *meditation*; knock in *prayer* and it will be opened to you in *contemplation*.[6]
>
> Praying over the Scriptures makes for a most substantial prayer life. . . . It is the Bible that provides the best book for private prayer. The best way to feed prayer

is to ponder the words of Scripture. St. Teresa said, "Carmelites (in fact, all Christians) make a great mistake in trying to practice 'the presence of God' without sustaining it by the word of God. We need to learn to pray over God's word."[7]

A FINE ART

You can see from the above quotes that praying the Bible in community with other believers is neither new nor novel. It helps our prayer lives because it brings an entirely new focus to what we are praying about. In fact, for the early monks and nuns, praying the Scriptures was a centering device:

> Meditation seeks to acquire the mind of Christ. One slowly begins to see what the Scriptures are saying. The meditator begins the lifetime task of hearing the word of God, so as to keep it.[8]

Because they were so diligent at praying the Bible, the monastics of the Early Church and medieval Church transformed the practice of praying the Bible into a fine art. They broke down the command of Joshua 1:8—to meditate on the Law—into four distinct elements, which later became widely known as the *lectio divina:*

> [The] lectio itself, which means 1) "reading," understood as the careful repetitious recitation of a short text of Scripture; 2) meditation or "meditation," an effort to fathom the meaning of the text and make it personally relevant to oneself in Christ; 3) oratio, which means "prayer," taken as a personal response to the text, asking

for the grace of the text or moving over it toward union with God; and 4) contemplation, translated "contemplation," gazing at length on something. The idea behind this final element is that sometimes, by the infused grace of God, one is raised above meditation to a state of seeing or experiencing the text as a mystery and reality; one comes into experiential contact with the One behind and beyond the text. It is an exposure to the divine presence, to God's truth and benevolence.[9]

The *lectio divina* was practiced everywhere in Christendom for hundreds of years both in community and privately. Even Martin Luther did this, as he shared in a letter to a friend:

> I will tell you as best I can what I do personally when I pray. . . . First, when I feel that I have become cool and joyless in prayer because of other tasks or thoughts (for flesh and the devil always impede and obstruct prayer), I take my little psalter, hurry to my room . . . and, as time permits, I say quietly to myself and word-for-word the Ten Commandments, the Creed, and, if I have time, some words of Christ or of Paul, or some Psalms, just as a child might do.[10]

The same is true of revivalist George Whitefield. Whitefield, a contemporary and good friend of John Wesley, was undoubtedly the greatest preacher of what has historically been called the first Great Awakening. Like many of those before him, Whitefield discipled himself by praying the Bible. When he was 21 years old, he came upon salvation by faith in Christ's saving work alone. The evidence of his new birth was immediately apparent from both his now famous *Journals* and *Diary*. As soon as he was saved, he began to measure his day with a list of 15 criteria. Here are some questions he used to formulate his criteria:

1. Have I been fervent in private prayer?
2. Have I used stated hours of prayer?
3. Have I used ejaculation (vocal prayer) every hour?[11]

Historian Arnold Dallimore recounts:

His Diary shows his unyielding adherence to his "stated hours of prayer," first thing in the morning, again at noon and finally at night. . . .

Again his words conjure up a picture in the mind. There he is at five in the morning, in the room above the Harris bookstore. He is on his knees with his English Bible, his *Greek New Testament* and Henry's *Commentary* spread out before him. He reads a portion in the English, gains a fuller insight into it as he studies words and tenses in the Greek and then considers Matthew Henry's explanation of it all. Finally, there comes the unique practice he has developed: that of "praying over every line and word" of both the English and the Greek till the passage, in its essential message, has veritably became part of his own soul. . . .

When, in later chapters, we see him preaching forty and more hours a week, with little or no time preparation, we may well look back on these days in Gloucester and recognize that he was laying up a store of Biblical knowledge on which he was able to draw amidst the haste and tumult of such a ministry.[12]

When at 24 years old Whitefield began to preach daily to crowds of up to 40,000 at a time—all without amplification—his accomplishments were colossal. Dallimore believes that these crowds could have been the largest crowds ever addressed without the assistance of amplification.[13] No doubt, Whitefield's early practice in prayer had a lot to do with his later success in revival.

A LASTING TRADITION

We could go through history and give you example after example of Christians from every culture and century practicing this age-old art of praying the Bible. Right up to today, Christians who are experienced in prayer pray the Bible, as this testimony from executive vice president of Asian Outreach, David Wang, illustrates. Though David himself was Hong Kong Chinese, his training was largely Western. He himself noticed the contrast in prayer when he visited the underground Chinese Church in the 1980s:

> The [Chinese] sister then suggested that we should pray for one another. I was the only brother in the group, so following Chinese culture, I was asked to begin. I prayed longer than I usually do and used a heavy dose of pious vocabulary. I thought I was following the pattern of China's Church. And then it was Sister Yang's turn. In a most natural and free-flowing manner, she began to pray in the language of Scripture. Quoting from Romans to

Genesis to Philippians to the Psalms, Sister Yang used Scripture throughout her entire prayer of ten to fifteen minutes. She claimed God's promises using Scripture; she responded positively to God's call—again using Scripture. By the time Sister Yang had finished, we were awed! There was absolutely no pretentiousness on her part. It was all very natural and sincere.

Later as we shared this incident with others who have prayed with Chinese believers, we discovered that Sister Yang was not exceptional. A former China missionary said, "Even before I was forced out of China, I noticed that Chinese Christians prayed eloquently. And now when I return I hear not just the same eloquence, but often long passages of Scripture being prayed aloud by the believers."

She attributed this to the fact that for 30 years, Bibles have been in extremely short supply. For many of China's believers, the Word of God consists of what they have memorized from a borrowed Bible, or Scripture portion copied by hand. Scripture memorization comes naturally to them, partly due to practice and necessity, but also due to a love of the Word. "Often they pray through their entire theology," a scholar of a leading Chinese Christian research center commented. "They pray in Scripture language not only as a reinforcement of what they have memorized, but also as a verbalization of their theology—the way some do of the Apostle's Creed. But their repetition of Scriptures is personal and relevant to their current situation. We outsiders sometimes think that the person leading prayer is trying to sermonize. This may not be the case, for often believers pray through their theology in their private prayers as well."

Praying in Scripture language is actually being taught in a mushrooming house church movement in Henan province. I read in its hand-copied "Pastoral Care Manual" that using Scriptures in prayer is one certain way of praying according to the will of God. Our co-workers who have close contact with China's believers all feel we should learn this lesson—that praying in the language of God's Word brings God-glorifying results.[14]

You will notice from this example several benefits of praying the Bible. You will also notice the marked difference between David's flowery prayer and the Chinese believer's Scripture-based prayer. It is a common occurrence that when people don't know what to say, they pray the wrong stuff. A pastor we know tells the story of leading a prayer meeting where a young woman was praying all over the map. Finally, the pastor stopped her and asked her to pray Bible prayers so that everyone else could say "Amen." She responded by saying, "But I don't know any Bible prayers," to which the pastor replied, "I know, it shows." When a person does not know what to say, their prayers are often difficult to follow, let alone participate in. As that pastor said, we need to pray the Bible so that everyone else can say "Amen." As the Chinese believers did, we need to pray the Bible to reinforce and verbalize our theology. As the monks and nuns of old did, we need to pray the Bible as the means to experiential union with God. As the people in the Bible did, we need to pray the Bible in obedience to God's command.

BIBLE PRAYERS ARE
EASY TO FIND

A few years ago, we were ministering in the mountains of Puebla, which is about a four-hour drive from Mexico City. The situation was most desperate. The Indians of the area lived in villages built atop mountain peaks a mile high in the air, which meant that in order to get water, the villagers had to walk a mile straight down to the valley below. These villagers were descendants of the ancient Inca and Aztec tribes. Warring factions had driven these people to build on the very tops of the mountains in order to protect themselves from their enemies. Farming was difficult and life very harsh. Today alcoholism is rampant and violence and abuse are epidemic. It hardly seemed the place for two single Mexican *señoritas* to start church planting. Yet these two girls had braved the odds and seen scores of village Indians come to Christ and be baptized. At the end of one long day of preaching, one of these young church planters came up to me to give a testimony. "You will not remember me," she said, "but I was in one of your meetings in Mexico City. At that conference you taught about praying the Bible. You were talking about the missionaries of old and how the Celtic monks prayed the whole book of Psalms every week. Since the conference was called 'The Revolution,' you told us to 'pray the whole book of Psalms every week, for a number of months, and a revolution will take place in your

> PRAY THE WHOLE BOOK OF PSALMS EVERY WEEK, FOR MONTHS, AND A REVOLUTION WILL HAPPEN.

life.'" Beaming, she continued, "I began to do this. Six months later I gave up my practice as an accountant and here I am. I wouldn't be doing anything else. Thank you for teaching me to pray the Bible." Driving down from the mountains that night, I realized afresh the power of praying the Bible. It changes the lives of those who do it and the lives of those they touch.

Praying the Bible also works for children. Our friends in Dallas, Texas, heard this message on praying the Bible and began to implement it immediately. Their son, John-Samuel, was only 19 months old at the time. Within the month, he could pray the entire vision of the heavenly throne room in Revelation 4. By 22 months, it was his common practice. By 24 months, it was time to move on and find some new prayers from the Bible. We underestimate what children are capable of.

Specifically, where do we begin? Although any section of the Bible will work, if we are going to pray the Bible, the easiest place to start is with the recorded prayers. There are at least eight genres of biblical prayers:

- Theophanies—Visions of God
- The Psalms
- Prayers of Wisdom
- The Song of Songs
- Prayers of the Prophets
- The Prayers of Jesus
- Apostolic Prayers
- Hymns of the Revelation

In our previous book, *Praying the Bible: The Book of Prayers*, we provide 88 prayers comprised from these eight different genres.

We also provide detailed definitions of each of the genres, as well as instructions on how to pray them. However, for our purposes here, we will simply give a cursory explanation of the eight genres (see appendix B for a list of the 88 biblical prayers of the eight genres).

THEOPHANIES

The theophanies are the "visions of God" (Ezek. 1:1) recorded in Scripture (see chapter 4). We encourage people to begin praying the Bible by praying the theophanies, because in doing so, they will start all their prayers by praying *to God* as He has revealed Himself. They will gain a much fuller understanding of who He is in their prayer life, which will undoubtedly increase their faith, since they will understand that they are praying to the One who has all the power in heaven and Earth to answer their cries. After all, God is who He says He is, not who we think He is. Praying the theophanies will keep us from praying to an extension of our own darkened minds.

THE PSALMS

The book of Psalms has historically been the prayer book of the Church. The New Testament states that if you are filled with the Spirit, then praying the Psalms will be a natural outcome (see Eph. 5:17-20). All followers of God prayed the Psalms (see Acts 2:42; Col. 3:16; Jas. 5:13), and the Church has continued this practice for 2,000 years. It is a brilliant place to start if you are just learning how to pray the Bible.

By praying the Psalms, you will have language to express the feelings of your heart to God. David wrote the majority of the Psalms, and he based them on his experiences on the battlefield, his hardships and his delights. He produced a language of worship and warfare for communicating with God. A simplistic view might break the Psalms down into three or four categories. First, the "I love you, I love you, I love you" psalms of worship and devotion. Second, the "I love you, and I'm sorry I blew it" psalms of repentance. Third, the "I love you, but I'm in trouble" psalms of petition and intercession. If we wanted to consider a fourth, it would be the "Help! Now get 'em God" imprecatory psalms. When you pray the Psalms, you are praying the words of a man after God's own heart—words full of the emotion and pathos of everyday life. In the Psalms, there are words to express your heart in virtually every situation you may find yourself in, whether you are overwhelmed with sorrow or filled with joy. When you say these words to God, you will become increasingly aware that God truly cares about all that you are going through. His eyes really are on the sparrow (see Ps. 84:3), and His eyes are on you.

PRAYERS OF WISDOM

Technically, there is no such thing as wisdom prayers. However, there is wisdom literature that can be shaped into prayer. Forming the wisdom of Proverbs and Ecclesiastes into prayers is great for those just beginning to pray, because the content deals with the issues of how to live life well. Such prayers will help us live our ordinary lives with the supernatural insight that comes from the source of wisdom—"the only wise God" (1 Tim. 1:17; Jude 1:25, *KJV*). With each of the genres of biblical prayer, there are different aspects that can be learned about who God is and how He views the world. By praying the wisdom prayers, you will see that wisdom is understood as the proper application of spirituality to daily life. You will learn that God cares about the practical side of life as well as the spiritual. You pray wisdom prayers by first picking a topic, such as wisdom, work, speech, sex, mercy, virtue, leadership or relationships. Then do a small word study by arranging as many verses together on that particular subject as you feel comfortable praying. These are the prayers that will make for a wise son and a good father, and a wholesome daughter and a noble wife. The words of Proverbs and Ecclesiastes will teach you how to excel in this temporal life and the internal disciplines that make for true success.

THE SONG OF SONGS

The Song of Songs, for many people, is somewhat confusing as a prayer book. For those who understand the mystical symbolism of the book, however, it becomes the book in the Bible which provides language for intimate communion with God. Although we understand the distinction between its literal and allegorical interpretations, we also recognize that throughout the Bible, God calls both Israel and the Church His Bride, and compares apostasy with adultery and even divorce. In the New Testament, Paul likens the earthly counterpart of sexual union—becoming one flesh—to the spiritual realities of salvation (see Eph. 5:31-32). Jesus is the Bridegroom and we are His Bride. In the same way, the words depicting the erotic relationship of Solomon and the Shulamite in the Song of Songs can be used in prayer in a symbolic way to describe our spiritual union with God. When we pray the words of the Song of Songs, we learn a secret love language for communicating with God in a bridal love paradigm.

PRAYERS OF THE PROPHETS

The prayers of the prophets deal with man in crisis. Job said, "Yet man is born to trouble as surely as sparks fly upward" (Job 5:7). Therefore, the prayers in this section of the Bible are cries that arise when there are real enemies, armies or terrorists. The prophets tended to look at nations or situations from a divine standpoint; many of them lived in the nations or were near the situations that they were prophesying about. Because they heard the prophetic words and because they lived in the middle of the circumstance, the people in the prophet sections of the Bible prayed with great fervor. For example, Daniel's prayer for the nation of Israel in Daniel 9 is a prototype of the heart of a prophet for his nation. Although he clearly knew from God why Israel was under judgment, he stood in the gap, and from the middle of the crisis, he asks God for forgiveness and mercy. Whether your situations are corporate—as in Daniel's prayer— or individual—as in Hezekiah's prayer (see 2 Kings 19:15-19)— you will learn what to say to God when you are facing adversity or blessing.

THE PRAYERS OF JESUS

When you pray the prayers of Jesus, you are engaging in the highest form of discipleship. By praying the words of Jesus, we enter His mind and Spirit, and soon His concerns become our concerns. As this happens, we can then begin to apply the prayers to similar situations in our own lives. The classic Lord's Prayer, or Our Father, is the most complete and most prayed prayer in all of history; it covers all of life. Going deeper in prayer, we can pray for our own families, friends and loved ones in the same way that Jesus prayed for His disciples in John 17. His concerns for His disciples were for protection and unity (see vv. 11-12), for joy in the midst of a hostile world (see vv. 13-16) and for practical holiness cultivated by the Word (see vv. 17-19). It is a small step for any committed Christian to turn these classic texts into primary concerns for his or her own disciples. We can also ask the Father directly for the same things that Jesus did. When we do this, it slowly begins to dawn on us that the things that Jesus did we are also to do:

> A pupil is not above his teacher; but everyone, after he has been fully trained, will be like his teacher (Luke 6:40, *NASB*).

Praying Jesus' prayers imbues our spirits with the understanding that the whole of our lives are to be patterned after the whole of His life. We are to imitate His life here on Earth.

APOSTOLIC PRAYERS

The apostolic prayers are some of the most unique prayers in the Bible. Paul was as advanced and sophisticated as a man could be with respect to being trained in the Book of the Law. He describes himself as being "a Hebrew of Hebrews" (Phil. 3:5). According to the strictest sect of Judaism, Paul said he lived as a Pharisee (see Acts 26:5). In regard to righteousness based on the Law, he was faultless (see Phil. 3:6). When it came to zeal for his cause, Paul describes himself as advancing in Judaism beyond many Jews of his own age (see Gal. 1:14). Add to that the fact that Paul had a highly dominant personality and a brilliant mind. With this as his foundation, Paul had a supernatural encounter with the very One he was persecuting—the risen

Christ (see Acts 9:3-9; 26:12-18). Following this encounter, instead of killing the followers of the Way, Paul began to lay down his own life for them.

The prayers that Paul prays for his disciples and the churches he plants are some of the richest, most meaty prayers in the Bible. Paul has a thorough understanding of the Law, grace, the Church and holy living. He is the father of the Church and eminent teacher of theology. His apostolic prayers mainly focus on three things: gifts, fruit and wisdom. His prayers for gifts have to do with the release of the ministry gifts of the Holy Spirit, to the point where revival breaks out on account of our ministry and the ministry of our fellow workers. His prayers for fruit are a plea for godly character to be manifested in our lives. Finally, his prayers for wisdom are about knowing all that we can about God. It is receiving the fascinated heart in which we can search out the mysteries and knowledge of God so that we may know him better. This threefold prayer request for gifts, fruit and wisdom is all unto the glory of God so that His kingdom come and His will be done in our churches, cities and regions.

HYMNS OF THE REVELATION

Sometimes people wonder what they are going to do for eternity in heaven. Who will be there? What will they say to God when they see Him face-to-face? Praying the hymns of the Revelation provides a sneak preview of what those who are before the very face of God do and say. It also provides a head start on doing it here on Earth before you get to heaven. When you pray the hymns of the Revelation, you can pray with all of heaven, going before God as He sits on His throne to join with Him in worship. You will hear some of the very words the angels and elders say to God, and you get to say what they say with them. The hymns show us some of what is going on in heaven, what will happen when heaven comes here and how all of heaven and Earth talk to the One on the throne and to the Lamb.

Praying the hymns gives you a glimpse into perfection. Obviously, heaven's perspective on life is quite different from Earth's. The hymns reveal that those in heaven are totally jubilant and victorious, no matter how terrible the circumstances on Earth may be. Even during the end-time judgments, there is no sorrow in heaven, only praise, that at last God has taken His great power and begun to reign.

YOU WILL PRAY THINGS YOU HAVE NEVER PRAYED BEFORE

Before we close this chapter, we want to remind you of the benefits of praying the Bible. As we already mentioned, praying the Bible leads you to places in God that you never would have discovered otherwise:

> As the heavens are higher than the earth, so are my ways higher than your ways and my thoughts than your thoughts (Isa. 55:9).

During a visit to Lanceston, Tasmania, several years ago, the locals told us to be sure to take a walk up the river pathway. When we did, we were astounded by the beauty. With every turn there was a new cliff or gorge, or something breathtaking. As we walked back, we were amazed to think that we never even knew such a place existed, yet it was there all along. Similarly, whether it is an apostolic prayer or a theophany, praying the words of the Bible will take you to places you never would have gone on your own. It's like turning onto a new, unknown road—you're going to see sights you have never seen before.

YOU CAN LEARN THE LANGUAGE OF REPENTANCE

One place that all of us will go to at some point when we pray the Bible is the place of repentance:

"We all stumble in many ways," says James (Jas. 3:2).

Since no one is perfect, we will eventually all find ourselves at this place. When we pray the Bible, we will find words that help to express repentance. While biblical repentance is not full of guilt and condemnation, it does take ownership for wrongs done.

I was once in the Philippines speaking on prayer. The Philippines have the distinction of being the first Christianized country of Southeast Asia. Magellan came there from Spain, and within a short period of time, the whole nation converted to Catholicism. I asked the crowd, "How many of you used to go to confession and the priest would tell you to pray 10 Our Fathers and 5 Hail Marys?" Large numbers of Filipinos put up their hands. Then I asked, "What were the priests trying to accomplish in giving you this exercise?" "Penance," replied the crowd. The idea of penance or punishment was clearly understood by all those who had ever done the exercise.

However, having had five children, I suggested that perhaps there is a different origin to this practice. I explained that

Canadian children are not as well behaved as children in other countries. Canadian children tend to fight a lot and often don't listen to their parents like children from the Philippines, who are better listeners. The parents chuckled and the children squealed with delight. I continued, "This is what happens in our house in Canada. From time to time, I will hear loud screams, thuds and then more mayhem coming up from the basement, until finally the youngest boy comes up crying loudly, tears streaming down his cheeks. 'What's going on? Why are you crying?' I ask. Through sobs, Simeon says, 'Joab punched me.' 'Joab—get up here! Joab, did you punch Simeon?' Hearing the angry tone in my voice, he silently nods yes. 'Why did you punch Simeon?' 'Well, Simeon kicked me in the leg!' 'Simeon, did you kick Joab in the leg?' 'Yes,' he sobs. 'Why did you kick Joab?' 'Because he poked me in the stomach.' 'Joab, did you poke Simeon in the stomach?' 'Yes!' 'And why did you poke him in the stomach?' 'I poked him because he was touching me.' 'Simeon, were you touching him?' 'Yes, but he was on my side of the couch and I was telling him to get on his own side.' To which Joab protests, 'No, I was not on your side, you were on my side, and you were touching me, and so I pushed you!' Exasperated, I shout, 'Stop it! Nobody is to touch anybody—in all the world— ever again! You, Joab, go in that room and give me three Psalm 51s. You, Simeon, go in that room and give me five Beatitudes from Matthew 5! Now go and pray, and ask God for the power to get along and be nice!'"

Alas, such scenes actually do take place in our home. Through such scenes, however, we have found that prayers at times like this are not given as punishment but as language to repent with. The Bible gives us words that are not full of blame and guilt but contrition and responsibility. Once we have found language to repent with, we can then ask for the right heart to move forward with.

AN AUTHORITY WE DON'T HAVE IN OURSELVES

Another benefit of praying the Bible is that it makes you enter the throne of grace with new boldness, because you know that you are praying according to God's will:

> This is the confidence we have in approaching God: that if we ask anything according to his will, he hears us. And if we know that he hears us—whatever we ask—we know that we have what we asked of him (1 John 5:14-15).

Instead of hoping to receive answers to our prayers, we can be assured—based on the promises of God—that prayers prayed according to His will will be answered. Your faith will be strengthened, your wisdom will become spiritual wisdom and your knowledge of God will increase.

For a time we were really into praying the hymns of the Revelation. One time we doted on Revelation 11:15-18:

> The seventh angel sounded his trumpet, and there were loud voices in heaven, which said: "The kingdom of the world has become the kingdom of our Lord and of his Christ, and he will reign for ever and ever." And the twenty-four elders, who were seated on their thrones before God, fell on their faces and worshiped God, saying:

"We give thanks to you, Lord God Almighty, the One who is and who was, because you have taken your great power and have begun to reign. The nations were angry; and your wrath has come. The time has come for judging the dead, and for rewarding your servants the prophets and your saints and those who reverence your name, both small and great—and for destroying those who destroy the earth."

Having never prayed this before, we had no idea how strong the words were. Who would ever ask for such things? Yet praying the Bible gave us authority because it is God's Word that we were speaking. Soon we were all shouting Revelation 11:18 with uncharacteristic boldness. Praying Bible prayers helped us be bold where we would not normally have been so bold.

You too can pray Revelation 11:17-18 in your own words, "And all heaven gave thanks that by Your power You have begun to reign. It is time for destroying those who destroy the earth. It is time to judge the living and the dead." Perhaps in your own self you would never be so bold as to say such things, but because it is the Bible, you can say it.

SPIRITUAL ALIGNMENT IS VERY IMPORTANT

Praying the Bible begins to disciple the intercessor into a biblical versus cultural worldview. As the Bible permeates our thinking, we will have a vantage point of the world, which is not egocentric, but rather Christcentric. Alignment is important. If our backs or necks get out of alignment, they can give us headaches and many other troubles. In order to get them back in alignment, we go to chiropractors and get them snapped back into place. Similarly, our thoughts can get out of alignment. We often think worldly, nonspiritual thoughts about ourselves and others. Really, how many of us go before God in the language of Psalm 18, the "battle hymn of the King"?

Some time ago, I began praying Psalm 18 because I liked the strong battle imagery. *I can run through a troop, leap over a wall and bend a bow of bronze. Aarrgghh, Braveheart!* Yes! Soon I found that it was one of my favorite prayers. Slowly, however, the true understanding of the context began to dawn on me. David is talking here about a real battle with real enemies that were about to kill him. He cried out for help when he was on the verge of being annihilated. God came to his rescue, and now David is singing about it. Why did God come? Simply because David was his son, his special one, his favorite. In the 50 verses of this Psalm, David uses "me," "my" and "I" 100 times. It's as though it's all about him and God. When you pray these verses and others like it, without realizing it, David's attitude will become your own. Suddenly you will begin to believe that you are God's favorite; you are His anointed one. God is for you; therefore, who can be against you? It's like a trip to the spiritual chiropractor.

Are we really conscious when we pray that God is for us and that we are His favorites? When you pray the Bible, you will understand how God views you and how He views others. In a culture distorted by negative media images, we all need to be founded on what God thinks of us. David's self-image came through prayer. He saw himself as God's anointed, as the apple of His eye. David knew that God loved him and that he was favored while the wicked were not. That's why God got him out of jams. Therefore, we need to pray the Bible until we have the same attitude that David had.

THE PASSION FOR JESUS IS CONTAGIOUS

The life of a Christian is all about passion for Jesus. Mike Bickle always says that it takes God to love God. Nothing is more powerful than the Holy Spirit's revelation of the Son of God through the words of Scripture. Like the disciples on the road to Emmaus, every heart began to burn when God revealed Himself. When He unveils Himself and we have understanding of what He is saying, passion is the result.

Seeking the face of God, and then gazing at it, has to begin sometime and someplace. It begins by bringing our whole person before the consuming fire who is God, reciting His words, the Bible, out loud to Him and then letting the Holy Spirit reveal Christ to us. This is why we pray the Bible. May it be that as you engage in this practice, your prayer times will have the same result as the disciples, whose hearts burned within as God talked with them along their journey of life. Yes, may your heart burn and your light shine.

CHAPTER SIX

PRAYING OUT LOUD

Developing Kavvanah

When traveling abroad, a Westerner will most likely discover that the rest of the world is not like him. Like Galileo's discovery that the sun does not revolve around the earth, it is sometimes a shock when the Western world realizes that not all people think the way they do, or that perhaps their way is not the best way. This is especially true in regard to prayer. The rest of the world does not pray like Westerners. They mostly pray out loud and loudly—all at the same time—while they move or walk around. Westerners usually pray sitting down—one at a time, relatively softly, devoid of emotion.

Well over 20 years ago, I remember sitting in my tent in the middle of the African bush. Night after night, I would hear the Nigerians saying their prayers, all alone in their tents. This little Canadian in the villages of Nigeria was already experiencing culture shock, but to hear them pray intensified it. I thought, *Why do they pray out loud when no one else is in the room?* I found it very strange indeed. Then I went to their large church gatherings where thousands of Nigerians would congregate. When the leader said, "Let's pray," the whole place erupted with everyone all at once praying very loudly. Since this was my first overseas mission trip, I dismissed it as a cultural thing—a Nigerian phenomenon.

However, years later we traveled to Korea. It was the same there. Everyone prayed out loud, simultaneously. We went to their "Prayer Mountain" where hundreds of "prayer grottos," little four-foot cubicles encased in cement, were dug out of the side of the mountain. Individual Koreans would shut themselves into these prayer grottos, and there, alone before God, they prayed out loud. As we walked by closed door after closed door, we could hear the rising and falling of their voices calling out to God. In time, we traveled to over 50 countries and regions including China, India, Latin America and Southeast Asia, where we always found the same practice of prayer. It was only in the Western countries that people prayed differently. The rest of the world prays out loud and loudly. Why?

THE GOAL OF PRAYER

The goal of prayer is not merely to *say* our prayers. The Desert Father, Saint Cassian, said, "The man who prays only when on his knees, prays little. The man who kneels to pray and then lets his mind wander, prays not at all.[1] Ultimately, our goal is friend-ship with God. Showing up is good, but if all we do after that is merely pray as the hypocrites and Pharisees pray, we have obvi-ously lost the point.

Thus far, everything that has been discussed in this book has been to provide building blocks for a stairway to God's pres-ence. Now we have arrived at the top of the staircase and we have gotten to the most important part: touching God. The writer to the Hebrews says:

> During the days of Jesus' life on earth, he offered up prayers and petitions with loud cries and tears . . . and he was heard because of his reverent submission (Heb. 5:7).

The obvious question is, Does this mean that we have to pray real loud and cry a lot in order to be heard? Though the answer is, not necessarily, the implication is that people cannot pray real loud or cry a lot unless they are really into it. Jesus was emotionally engaged in His prayer. He wept and sweat great drops of perspiration because He was emotionally impacted as He prayed (see Luke 22:44). He called out loudly because He was not praying from His head but from His heart. Most of us, how-ever, are so unimpassioned about what we are praying that we seldom experience an emotional flutter—let alone tears.

EXPERIENCING *KAVVANAH*

Mining the Jewish rabbinical tradition for resources on prayer can yield many profitable insights, since Christian tradition and rabbinical tradition have the same roots. They both tie back into the experience of God's people in the Hebrew Bible, the Old

Testament. Jesus and the New Testament writers were steeped in this tradition, as was the Early Church, who were mostly Jewish believers in Jesus. One caution is in order, however: The rabbinical tradition—originally an oral tradition—was written down by Jewish scholars living in Israel beginning sometime around A.D. 200. In other words, the Talmud and the Mishnah were formed during a time after the majority of the Jewish community had settled on not receiving Jesus as Messiah. Therefore, even though we as Christians can learn from and appreciate the rabbinical tradition, for us it is not authoritative.

One of the rabbinical insights that we as Christian believers can affirm is the idea of *kavvanah;* that is, when a person is so touched by the Spirit of God that not only are the person's words prayer, but also he or she "becomes prayer." This "becoming prayer," or touching God and becoming one with his purposes and desires, ought to be our goal in prayer.

In order to obtain this goal, people of faith use different resources in order to obtain kavvanah. For example, the Catholic tradition uses the stations of the cross. Praying through the stations is a way of going on a pilgrimage to the scene of Christ's crucifixion without going to Jerusalem. The stations of the cross is also a way for the pilgrim to enter empathetically into what is called the "Passion of Christ," which is what Christ's love for the Father and for the Church impelled Him to do by going to the Cross for us. Usually found inside or on the grounds of a Catholic church, the stations are 14 plaques, pictures or carvings that depict the arrest and trial of Jesus, the guards beating Him, the gruesome parade where Jesus was forced to carry His own cross, small acts of mercy given to Jesus during that parade and finally His crucifixion. At each station—usually just a few paces from each other—the pilgrim prays and meditates on what Jesus has done for him or her, and what he or she can do for Jesus in return.

Protestant churches use a resource called the *Book of Common Prayer*, which has been around for nearly 500 years. Forming its roots from the Anglican and Episcopalian traditions, the *Book of Common Prayer* helps believers in the following ways:

- Praying the Bible—the prayers in the *Book of Common Prayer* are saturated with Scripture, many are lifted word for word from Scripture.
- Praying through the Psalms—there are several ways the *Book of Common Prayer* gives you for praying through the Psalms.
- Praying out loud—the *Book of Common Prayer* is intended to be read aloud. It is good for individuals or groups.
- Praying morning, noon and night—there is an order of worship for mornings, noontimes and evenings.
- Praying as an individual, with families or small groups, or in larger settings—the *Book of Common Prayer* can be used for personal individualized prayer and for various sizes of groups.
- Praying daily—the *Book of Common Prayer* Old Testament and New Testament readings are calibrated to help a person read through most of the Bible in a two-year period. In this way, the Psalms form the backbone of the whole enterprise of prayer in the *Book of Common Prayer*, but the Bible as a whole is honored.
- Praying themed passages—these passages focus on Advent, Lent, Holy Week and Pentecost, which are the

periods of the Church year that are most conducive to meditating on what God has done for us in Christ.

The rabbis have always taught that there are different levels of kavvanah as well as specific methods to create it. The basic level is understanding the text being prayed. From there, the worshiper can move to identification. The Talmud describes how certain sages recited the words, "He lets the winds blow," and instantly the winds began to blow, and when they recited, "He lets the rains fall," the rains began to fall. This would be akin to miracle workers or faith healers. Somehow they have so entered into their prayer that their words connect with God's words, and as they pray or speak His holy intentions, miracles and wonders actually occur. Jesus experienced the creative power of the Father when He identified with the wretched condition of the people of His day, and also with how God wanted to touch them. The gospel of Matthew says:

> When he saw the crowds, he had compassion on them, [or better yet, 'the inner bowels of his emotions were moved'] because they were harassed and helpless, like sheep without a shepherd (Matt. 9:36).

Jesus touched these crowds and healed everyone (see Matt. 4:24; 9:35; 14:14; 15:30; 19:2). The fact that hundreds and even thousands of disciples since the time of Jesus have moved in similar power (e.g., Peter, Philip, Paul, Saint Antony, Francis of Asissi, John G. Lake, Maria Woodsworth-Etter, Smith Wigglesworth, Aimee Semple McPherson and Benny Hinn) proves that the healing power was not due entirely to the fact that Jesus was the Son of God. No, it was something that He modeled in His prayer that had creative power; it was something others also could follow in their prayer lives. It was kavvanah, or the power of identification, in His prayers that resulted in the creative power to heal every disease and sickness (see Matt. 9:35).

Whatever the Jewish rabbis said about how to enter into kavvanah seems to have consistently been passed down to God's people through the centuries, because each century has come up with the same recipe: Pray out loud! Why? Because there is always an ever-present danger of slipping into boring, non-heartfelt prayer. The rabbis warned, "Prayer without kavvanah is like a body without a soul."[2] Rabbi Steinsaltz says that the three fixed daily prayer times are based on the biblical verse:

> But I call to God, and the LORD saves me. Evening, morning and noon I cry out in distress, and he hears my voice (Ps. 55:16-17).[3]

The rabbis discovered an interesting paradox: The two things that diminish kavvanah the most are the very two things that God prescribes—set times of prayer and praying from a fixed text. In other words, daily prayer from a text can easily become lifeless tradition. Therein is both the strength and the possible weakness of the structure for prayer. Showing up allows for the possibility of connecting with God; the text provides the language to speak to Him. However, silent prayer can cause the mind to wander and the emotions of many to dissipate. Therefore, praying the text out loud is a bridge between the two.

FINDING THE SPIRIT

Africans understand this problem of getting into the Spirit. Recently, I met with a dynamic leader and a good friend of ours, Bishop Jackson Khosa, from South Africa. He pastors in the center of one of the most violent sections of the Johannesburg townships. During the scourge of apartheid, his life was threatened many times. He emerged through the adversity as a real apostle to thousands of young black leaders. One night he took me into the center of the township to an old dilapidated school building, which had been used as a base for murder, rape and violence. Today the place is a House of Prayer. I was to preach that night in the middle of the township. After he heard me preach on praying the Bible, he said excitedly, "This is it! This is what we must preach everywhere—to all the churches. This is how to achieve *emoyeni.*" Knowing I had just missed something important, I asked, "What is emoyeni?" "Oh," he said with a gleam in his eye, all the while moving his hands in a circular motion in front of him, like water tumbling over a waterfall, "emoyeni is getting into the Spirit! It is getting to where we want to be in God." Laughing, he added, "You white guys, you go to church and think you have arrived. We Africans, we go to church so that together we can get to the place we are going. Our purpose in going to church is to achieve emoyeni. Showing up at church is not the end; it is the beginning." I knew instinctively what he meant.

Jokingly he continued, "Every black man knows where he wants to go. And I guarantee you, when we get there, we will stay longer than you. You white guys are busy with so many things—your computers and your businesses. You have too much to do here on Earth. For us, what else are we going to do? We have nothing here. Where we want to be is in the Spirit, and that is where our riches are. But you—even if you get to that place—will run out again too quickly, but we will stay there for a long time." With that, his big, bald head began bobbing up and down as he laughed and laughed. Slapping me heartily on the back, he knew he had me.

Most cultures have a specific word to describe the state they are trying to achieve, the state of being fully engaged in the presence of God. Whatever label we give it—kavvanah, emoyeni or "in the Spirit"—it's all the same thing. Obviously, spontaneous times of prayer have kavvanah, because they are born out of a sense of urgency, which supersedes the need for fixed times or for set texts. However, there must also be a way to develop kavvanah while we are obeying the injunction to pray at a set time with a set text. As mentioned earlier, most non-Western nations agree that the most effective way to pray is out loud. Among believers, it is virtually a universal understanding from all cultures, from every continent, through all the ages.[4]

> DO YOU KNOW WHY YOU SHOULD PRAY OUT LOUD? SO THAT YOU WILL KNOW WHEN YOU'VE STOPPED!

That's why we always ask our audiences the same basic question: Do you know why you should pray out loud? Pausing for impact and so everyone can search for some superspiritual answer, I answer my own question, "So you know when you've stopped!" It usually takes about 5 or 10 seconds for this statement to make its way from the ear to comprehension. However, slowly, they all begin to break into smiles . . . ha . . . uhhah . . . ha. Even though this sounds ridiculous, praying out loud actually does solve the problem of the wandering mind. Remember, it's hard to think about something

> USE YOUR MOUTH TO LASSO YOUR MIND, TO AFFECT YOUR HEART.

else while you're talking. Use your mouth to lasso your mind, to affect your heart. The tongue has the power to drag your whole body toward the fire of God, so you can feel the heat.

THE WANDERING MIND

Of course God had this all figured out from the beginning. The antidote for the malady of the wandering mind is prescribed in the very primitive structure given by God to Joshua. God ordered everyone to "*meditate* on it [the Law] day and night" (Josh. 1:8, emphasis added). Most of us have interpreted the word "meditate" as something that we do silently. Some understand it in the context of Eastern religions, where meditation involves the emptying of one's self to achieve some sort of *nirvana* (nothingness). All of this is a gross misunderstanding of what the word "meditate" means. One of the basic rules of biblical interpretation is to compare a word according to how it is used and translated in different contexts.

HAGAH

What exactly is biblical meditation? Strong's definition of the Hebrew word *hagah* means: "to imagine, meditate, mourn, mutter, roar, speak, study, talk, utter."[5] The International Standard Bible

Encyclopaedia interprets it as "to murmur," "to have a deep tone," "to sigh" and "to moan"; and *higgayon* means "the murmur or dull sound of the harp."[6] Patrick Miller, professor of Old Testament at Princeton University, writes concerning the root hagah:

> Virtually all of the instances of such meditating are in the Psalter and thus in the context of prayers. This may or may not be a musing in silence. Presumably in some cases it is. But the verb *hagah* often refers to a speaking act, and so the meditation in this instance may be verbal. At times, it seems to be accompanied by moaning and groaning (77:3). . . . Such meditation is not generalized or empty thinking. This is biblical meditation.[7]

When we compare the various nuances of hagah as it is translated throughout the Bible, we find some surprising synonyms. The traditional understanding of hagah is translated as "meditate," which appears in various Scriptures (see Josh. 1:8, Pss. 1:2; 63:8; 77:12; 143:5; Isa. 33:18). However, there are also many other ways the word "hagah" can be used:

To Imagine
"Why do the nations conspire and the peoples [hagah] plot ["imagine"—*KJV*; "devise"—*NASB*] in vain?" (Ps. 2:1; see also Ps. 38:12).

To Mourn
"I cried like a swift or thrush, I [hagah] moaned ["mourn"—*KJV*] like a mourning dove" (Isa. 38:14; see also Isa. 16:7).

To Mutter
"For your hands are stained with blood, your fingers with guilt. Your lips have spoken lies, and your tongue [hagah] mutters

wicked things" (Isa. 59:3). "When men tell you to consult mediums and spiritists, who whisper and [hagah] mutter, should not a people inquire of their God?" (Isa. 8:19).

TO ROAR

"This is what the LORD says to me: 'As a lion [hagah] growls ["roars"—KJV], a great lion over his prey'" (Isa. 31:4).

TO SPEAK

"The mouth of the righteous man [hagah] utters ["speaks"—KJV] wisdom, and his tongue speaks what is just" (Ps. 37:30; see also Ps. 35:28; Prov. 8:7).

TO STUDY

"The heart of the righteous [hagah] weighs ["studies"—NKJV; "ponders"—NASB] its answers, but the mouth of the wicked gushes evil" (Prov. 15:28).

TO TALK

"My tongue will [hagah] tell of ["talk of"—KJV; "utter"—NASB] your righteous acts all day long, for those who wanted to harm me have been put to shame and confusion" (Ps. 71:24).

TO UTTER

"My lips will not speak wickedness, and my tongue will [hagah] utter ["mutter"—NASB] no deceit" (Job 27:4).

SIACH

Closely related to the verb "hagah"—to meditate—is *siach,* also translated as "to meditate" (see Pss. 104:34;119:15,23,48,78,148). Like hagah, siach is translated a number of different ways depending on its context. Also like hagah, siach usually includes vocal speech. Various other translations of the word "siach" include

1. Commune (see Ps. 77:6, *KJV*)
2. Complain (see Job 7:11; see also Ps. 77:3, *KJV*)
3. Pray (Ps. 55:17, *KJV*)
4. Speak or converse (see Judg. 5:10; Ps. 145:5, *KJV*)
5. Talk (see 1 Chron. 16:9; Ps. 119:27; Prov. 6:22, *KJV*)

What these contexts demonstrate is that while our modern understanding of meditation is quite narrow—focusing entirely on the inner discipline of "thinking intently upon"—the Hebrew understanding is much broader. The Hebrew definitions also include the aspect of how meditation is achieved, namely, through the oral recitation of the text. In the case of the command given to Joshua—to meditate upon the Book of the Law—we can be confident that the word "hagah" meant "to say over and over again by speaking, muttering or reciting as a prayer," in order that understanding of the Law might come.

AN ORAL CULTURE

When Joshua had received the command to meditate on the Law "day and night," he was living in an oral culture. The Hebrews had been slaves for generations, and therefore, they did not have a written language. The majority of the Israelites would not have been able to read any language at all. On top of that, none of those who were taught to read (whether Egyptian or, later, Hebrew) would have had the privilege of having their own private scroll of the Torah. Thus, how could the people be expected to meditate on the Law when they couldn't read and when they didn't have access to the Torah? The obvious answer is that they learned it orally.

They gathered the families together, and from the time the children could talk, the elders would teach them to chant the Book of the Law out loud until it was known by heart. This is the reason why every syllable of the Hebrew Scriptures was accompanied with a set of musical notations called *tropes*. Tropes allowed the entire Old Testament to be chanted in sing-song fashion, so as to assist in the process of memorization. Some of the Psalms and Proverbs are even structured as musical acrostics (see Ps. 119; Prov. 31), which also made memorization easier. Therefore, the entire Old Testament was structured in such a way that it could be chanted and easily remembered. It was a kind of ancient Hebrew rap, if you will.

> THE ENTIRE OLD TESTAMENT WAS STRUCTURED IN SUCH A WAY THAT IT COULD BE CHANTED IN SINGSONG FASHION, SO AS TO ASSIST IN THE PROCESS OF MEMORIZATION; IT WAS A KIND OF ANCIENT HEBREW RAP, IF YOU WILL.

CHANTING SCRIPTURE

Susan Haik Ventura is a brilliant Orthodox Jewess scholar from Paris. She wrote an entire book on this subject, and her thesis is that the Scriptures were written in a form to be memorized and prayed out loud by chanting. She devotes a good deal of the study to finding out exactly how the ancient Hebrew chanting sounded; and she has even reproduced on CD what she believes these chantings of the Psalms sounded like.[8] She believes that the Hebrew chanting of Psalms was a low, earthy, harmonious sound—unlike the present form that evolved from medieval times.[9] On this issue, we err if we do not appreciate the power of these mnemonic cultures.

PASSING THE LAW TO FUTURE GENERATIONS

We remember seeing this graphically played out in front of us. We were at the Holocaust Museum in Washington, D.C., walking through the section of Jewish history from the time of the early twentieth century. The movie footage looked like that of the era of the first World War. The presentation was highlighting Jews living in Eastern Europe, somewhere around Greece or Romania. Suddenly, we couldn't believe what we were seeing. There on the screen in black and white, with no audio sound, was an old, wizened Jew with his black hat and curls, leading six young boys in the chanting of the Book of the Law. He had a five-foot long switch in his hand that he deftly flicked toward any of the boys who seemed to be slacking off in their recitation. The boys were obviously into it, sitting cross-legged, bobbing back and forth at the waist and occasionally turning from side to side. Because we were cognizant of the prevalent oral culture of the time, we recognized

> DURING THE TIME OF JESUS, MANY JEWS COULD CHANT THE ENTIRE BOOK OF THE LAW, THE COMPLETE PSALMODY AND MANY OF THE SONGS OF THE PROPHETS.

what they were doing immediately. It took a lot of hard work and adult supervision to disciple the generations to the extent where they were actually able to recite large portions of Scripture by memory.

During the time of Jesus, many Jews could chant the entire Book of the Law, the complete Psalmody and many of the songs of the prophets.[10] Jews keen on learning the tradition could quote from memory the daunting three-inch thick Mishnah. The superzealous scholars could recite the entire Talmud—a massive series of 8 to 10 volumes about a foot and a half thick. It's hard for us to imagine that this was the way the Talmud was passed on for hundreds of years until it finally found its way into print in the mid-sixth century. When we comprehend that the average Jew of Jesus' day could pray from memory any number of a thousand verses out loud—much the same way today's teenagers can sing any contemporary song off the radio—we see the command to meditate on the Book of the Law in a whole new light.

ACTING OUT THE LAW

As the Hebrew people passed the commandments of God on to their children through oral recitation, they were also developing within themselves the power to do the Law as well. Children grew up praying the Bible out loud to God until the Law itself eventually took root in their hearts (see chapter 2). To this very day, Orthodox Jews still pray the Book of the Law out loud. They can be seen at the Wailing Wall or in synagogues, bobbing back and forth and rocking away as they mutter the Law. Their whole body is involved in the meditation. It is not merely a mental exercise or passive contemplation. No, it is an engaging recitation of a specific text to the Lord. As stated above, they are using their mouths to lasso their minds, to affect their spirits.

For our part, over the last decades, we have had to learn the art of praying the Bible. Saint Teresa of Avila says that the first lesson in learning to meditate is "to say one's vocal prayers with attention and affection."[11] We have to be attentive! The initial resolution to become involved in prayer begins in the mind. We cannot complain that we don't know where to start. Smith Wigglesworth said, "I begin in the flesh, and I end in the spirit." What he meant was that he began by faith, feeling nothing, and out of obedience did what God had called him to do. No doubt it was this practice that led him to say, "I am a thousand times bigger on the inside than I am on the outside." But, of course, he did not start with this inner depth; rather, it was cultivated over time.

> SMITH WIGGLESWORTH SAID, "I BEGIN IN THE FLESH, AND I END IN THE SPIRIT."

OUT LOUD WITH REPETITION

When you pray out loud, you will find yourself repeating your text over and over again. Many people have tried to explain the process. Madame Guyon's classic *Experiencing the Depths of Jesus Christ*, written from prison in France (c. 1685), is hailed as one of the greatest Christian writings of all time. Will Durant, in his 11-volume history of mankind, devotes many pages to Madame Guyon and her writings, especially this little book that shook the nation of France. Its impact was felt all the way to the throne of Louis XIV.[12] The reason for its profound impact lay in that it gave people a method of prayer. She writes at the beginning:

> I would like to address you as though you were a beginner in Christ, one seeking to know him. In so doing, let me suggest two ways for you to come to the Lord. I will call the first way "praying the scriptures;" the second way I will call "beholding the Lord" or "waiting in His presence."
>
> "Praying the scripture" is a unique way of dealing with the Scripture; it involves both *reading and prayer* (emphasis added).
>
> Here is how you should begin. Turn to the scripture; choose some passage that is simple and fairly practical. Next come to the Lord. . . . There, before him, read a small passage of scripture you have opened to. Be careful as you read. Take in fully, gently and carefully what you are reading. Taste it and digest it as you read. . . .
>
> In coming to the Lord by means of "praying the scriptures" you do not read quickly; you read very slowly. You do not move from one passage to another, not until you have sensed the very heart of what you have read. You may then want to take that portion of scripture that has touched you, and turn it into prayer.[13]

Like all the rest, Madame Guyon advised to pray the Bible.

OUR "GUYON" EXPERIENCE

By (holy) accident, Stacey began the practice laid out by Guyon in the first months of her salvation. She had never read the Bible before and couldn't understand it apart from praying through it very slowly, word by word. She jokingly says:

> When I first became a Christian, I felt like I was the only one in the whole church who had never read the Bible. And when I read it, I couldn't understand it. I began praying the Bible, simply because I was the dumbest one in church. Little did I know that this was my pathway to intimacy with God. I really started doing it only because of my embarrassment at being so biblically illiterate (see chapter 7).

I (Wesley), however, didn't understand this practice for another 10 years. In our case, what became obvious and was learned from the outset to one was not even close to being comprehended by the other. Even though we prayed together, we never really compared notes on our methods of private prayer; thus, we continued for 10 years thinking that one was praying the same way the other did. It wasn't until after the rebuke on prayer that I began to be serious about learning to pray. From the teaching of Mike Bickle, I understood that I had to pray the Bible. I began praying the Bible without really knowing what I was doing. But as Stacey and I began to understand the impact of what we were praying, we both made concerted efforts—no matter whether we were alone, at a corporate prayer time or during worship—to engage in the practice of biblical meditation. On any and every given day, all we needed was to pick up the Bible and start praying Bible prayers out loud to God. Initially, I didn't think it was working, except I would find that my excitement in God increased after doing this for about a half hour or so.

In time, I stumbled upon Revelation 4 and began to pray a "vision of God." After doing this for an extended period, I came to a place where I could "see" heaven in a matter of seconds if I closed my eyes and focused. I could see the throne, the sapphire sea, the four and twenty elders, the living creatures—everything.

I no longer needed to depend on how good the rest of the worship service was, the choice of songs or the "anointing" in the church. I could feel *kavvanah* or *emoyeni* on my own in just a few minutes. I loved praying this passage so much that I wanted to pray out the book of Revelation more and more.

One day, I made an incredible discovery. It hit me that all of heaven prays out loud—and loudly. Repeatedly throughout the book of Revelation, I found

> VIRTUALLY EVERY TIME ANYONE WAS DOING ANYTHING IN HEAVEN IT WAS BOTH OUT LOUD AND LOUDLY. PASSION IS AT THE ROOT OF EVERYTHING LOUD.

that every being in heaven is shouting or singing in a loud voice (see Rev. 5:12; 6:10). Virtually every time anyone is doing anything in heaven, it is both out loud and loudly. Over 22 times, John notes that the praise, prayers and declarations of the angels in heaven are with a loud voice. In heaven, speech is described as being like the roar of a lion, the sound of an ocean or a sound like thunder. The seven thunders of judgment are said to have "uttered their voices" (Rev. 10:3, *KJV*). That's when I asked myself the questions, Why is everything loud? What is the reason for the volume? Why do people and angels and living creatures sing, shout, praise and declare so loudly? Simply stated, the reason is passion! Passion is at the root of everything *loud*.

Loaded with that new discovery, I would face the wall or pace back and forth. I imagined myself before the heavenly throne. From amongst the great throng of heaven, I would begin to shout either the 10 worship words or the many victory chants like those recorded in Revelation (see Rev. 4:11; 5:12-13; 7:12; 11:15). I imagined that my voice was a trumpet and that each worship word or victory chant made a different sound in heaven. For example, the word "power" would sound different from "wealth." "Wisdom" would make a different sound from "strength." And "honor," "glory" and "praise" were distinct from "blessing," "thanks" and "dominion." Then, I would lift up my voice like a trumpet (see Isa. 58:1; Rev. 1:10) and send these worship notes into the courts of heaven. By shouting these worship words to Him, my praise was forming its own worship song.

Invariably, after just a few minutes of this heavenly praise, I would feel the presence of the Spirit of God. I would then begin to pray any one of the scores of Bible prayers, whether a theophany, a psalm, a prayer of Jesus, an apostolic prayer or a hymn from Revelation. Whatever I was feeling at the time, I prayed. If nothing grabbed me from one text, I would move on to another. In the early days, when I was scheduled to preach on a given text, I would paraphrase as much of the text as could possibly be made into a prayer. Then I would go to the two hour preservice prayer meeting. There I would hold up my text and begin to pray it out strongly to God. Over and over again, I would pray through every phrase out loud and with passion. If a word or phrase seemed to stick out, I would pause at that place and repeat it several times. Then I would continue and launch off the written text into a spontaneous expansion of a similar thought or topic.

Nothing could stop me while praying this way. Even if I didn't feel unction, I would continue to pray. Even if I were in a church meeting that felt totally cold, I resolved never to let a worship time pass me by without forcing myself to engage with God. Remembering the advice of Smith Wigglesworth, I determined to "begin in the flesh in order to end in the Spirit." I pushed myself to pray Bible prayers out loud. Walking, pacing, bobbing and standing, I dove into a text of Scripture and said it out loud to God.

My Recent Revelation

More recently, I have begun to sing my prayers, which is still out loud communication with God. Even though I feel like I can't really sing well, I am trying to expand into the Spirit-filled life, which, according to the Bible, results in singing and making melody in my heart to the Lord (see Eph. 5:18-19; Col. 3:16). As James said, "Is anyone happy? Let him sing songs of praise" (Jas. 5:13).

I work at this most often in corporate gatherings when a worship team carries the tune. Again I face the wall and begin to sing in one key—in a monotone fashion. Once I have found some sort of musical groove, I begin chanting Scripture after Scripture. In a very short time, I begin to feel the anointing of the Holy Spirit. This singing or declaration of praying in the gift of tongues is also an entirely legitimate form of devotional prayer. But since this book specifically concerns praying the Bible, tongues are beyond the scope of this study.

THE VOICE AND BODY CORRELATION

We should also take a moment to highlight the connection between the voice and the body when one is praying. To date, I have endeavored to teach people to pray the Bible in over 200 cities worldwide. For a practicum at the end, I always ask the congregation to rise out of their chairs so that they can start marching around the outside perimeter of the building with their Bibles in hand and practice praying the Bible out loud. As they walk and pray, we have our "Praying the Bible" instrumental music playing loud enough in the background so that the people are not afraid of their own voices. Consistently, I have found that every congregation will continue praying four to five times longer if they walk and pray out loud with a text. All that is needed is a little coaching and some encouragement to keep them moving in a circular fashion around the church. Yet if they remain sitting or standing silently, instead of pacing or marching around, rarely can I motivate a crowd to pray longer than a few minutes. Usually people who sit or stand in the background always begin to talk or disengage in some form or fashion very quickly. However, if I can get the group pacing, they can pray easily—with everyone fully engaged—for half an hour to an hour. Even those who have never prayed for 10 minutes out loud in their life will be surprised at how long they can pray.

SAINT TERESA ENCOURAGES US BY SAYING, "VOCAL PRAYER CAN SUSTAIN ANY KIND OF MEDITATIVE EFFORT."

We have found that the Western style of praying—one after another, sitting in chairs, with no adherence to scriptural prayers—is probably the worst form for any culture in any country of any age. Plainly, it doesn't work!

Therein lies one of the reasons why so many of us have experienced so little joy in prayer: We don't become absorbed enough to be emotionally touched. We generally just sit there and let someone else pray for us. Consequently, prayer is boring, meaningless and irrelevant. To get to a deeper level, we need to gain confidence and focus by praying out loud. Once again, Saint Teresa encourages us by saying, "Vocal prayer can sustain any kind of meditative effort."[14] And like most who attain the heights of prayer, she believed this could be learned.

Vain Repetition in Prayer

A word should be said about vain repetition. For our part, we repeat verses often and continuously when we pray. Even Jesus prayed the same prayers every day at the same time. He told a parable on importunity, where persistent and even repetitive prayer was applauded (see Luke 11:1). Sometimes I pray verses like Revelation 5:12 many times over.

Like the angels, I shout in a loud voice and sing:

> "Worthy is the Lamb, who was slain,
>> to receive power
>>> and wealth
>>>> and wisdom
>>>>> and strength
>>>>>> and honor and glory and praise!"

I repeat these seven staccato-like shouts over and over. With each new pass, I expound in declaration or song on the worthiness of Jesus Christ, the Son of God, to receive the fullness of every word in the text. He is worthy of wealth—worthy of all the gold and silver. He is worthy of all the wealth of this world and worthy of my wealth. On and on I go. Repetition is wonderful and very useful, as long as it is not mindless or without meaning. Jesus did not say that we could not repeat our prayers. His instruction was not to repeat them if we didn't mean them or if we were treating prayer as some sort of magical incantation, where if we say the phrase just right or repeat it 10 or 15 times we will get what we want. Instead, Jesus said:

> And when you pray, do not keep on babbling like pagans,
> for they think they will be heard because of their many
> words (Matt. 6:7).

Or as the *NKJV* translates, "do not use vain repetitions as the heathen do. For they think that they will be heard for their many words." Prayer is not a show. Jesus said not to pray showy prayers—devoid of heart and meaning—just because everybody else is. The key word is the adjective "vain" or *battologeo,* which carries the idea of a proverbial stammer or stutter (i.e., to prate tediously).[15] The prohibition is not against repetitive prayer but against legalistic, performance-based prayer that silently shouts to those watching, "Look at me, see how good I can pray!" It is not the amount or eloquence of the prayers but the state of the heart of the one praying them. When the state of the heart is passionate, the prayers will be like those of the living creatures in heaven:

Day and night they never stop saying: "Holy, holy, holy
is the Lord God Almighty, who was, and is, and is to
come" (Rev. 4:8).

When you are passionate, maybe like the living creatures, you
won't be able to stop yourself. Day and night . . . night and
day . . . you never stop! You will pray out as loudly as you can, as
much as you can. In fact, at times like this, your volume may even
become the thermometer of your spirit, gauging how hot you
are. Praying out loud is the pathway to receiving a burning heart.

CHAPTER SEVEN

SILENT CONTEMPLATION

There is a rare flower in the garden of Russian Orthodox spirituality called *The Way of the Pilgrim*, which clarifies the important principle of praying without ceasing or, in the famous words of Brother Lawrence, "practicing the presence of God."[1] The book itself was written by an anonymous nineteenth-century Russian peasant. Unable to work because of a disability, he became a pilgrim, wandering from place to place, seeking spiritual wisdom and knowledge. More specifically, he wanted to learn how to pray without ceasing as is commanded in 1 Thessalonians 5:17. His visits to churches and monasteries provided him with some advice on the benefits of prayer, but he still had no idea—in practical terms—how to pray without ceasing. No one could enlighten him. Finally, he found a spiritual adviser who had some experience in the matter of ceaseless prayer. This man told him to go into the woods and pray this simple prayer: *Lord Jesus Christ, Son of God, have mercy on me, a sinner.*

In his own words, listen to what happened to the pilgrim when he went to ask for spiritual advice:

"Be so kind, Reverend Father, as to show me what prayer without ceasing means and how it is learnt. I see you know all about these things."

He took my request kindly and asked me into his cell.

"Come in," said he, "I will give you a volume of the holy Fathers from which with God's help you can learn about prayer clearly and in detail."

We went into his cell and he began to speak as follows.

"The continuous interior Prayer of Jesus is a constant, uninterrupted calling upon the divine Name of Jesus with the lips, in the spirit, in the heart; while forming a mental picture of His constant presence, and imploring His grace, during every occupation, at all times, in all places, even during sleep. The appeal is couched in these terms, 'Lord Jesus Christ, have mercy on me.' One who accustoms himself to this appeal experiences, as a result, so deep a consolation and so great a need to offer the prayer always, that he can no longer live without it, and it will continue to voice itself within him of its own accord. Now do you understand what prayer without ceasing is?"

"Yes indeed, Father, and in God's name teach me how to gain the habit of it," I cried, filled with joy.

"Read this book," he said. "It is called *The Philokalia,* and it contains the full and detailed science of constant interior prayer, set forth by twenty-five holy Fathers."

"Is it then more sublime and holy than the Bible?" I asked.

"No, it is not that. But it contains clear explanations of what the Bible holds in secret and which cannot be easily grasped by our shortsighted understanding. . . . Listen now, I am going to read you the sort of instruction it gives on unceasing interior prayer."

He opened the book, found instruction by St. Simeon, the New Theologian, and read: "Sit down alone and in silence. Lower your head, shut your eyes, breathe out gently and imagine yourself looking into your own heart. Carry your mind (i.e., your thoughts) from your head to your heart. As you breathe out, say 'Lord Jesus Christ, have mercy on me.' Say it moving your lips gently, or simply say it in your mind. Try to put all other thoughts aside. Be calm, be patient, and repeat the process very frequently. . . . "

I learned that there was a village between two and three miles from the monastery. I went there to look for a place to live, and to my great happiness God showed me the thing I needed. A peasant hired me for the whole summer to look after his kitchen garden and, what is more, gave me the use of a little thatched hut in it where I could live alone. God be praised that I had found a quiet place. And in this manner I took up my abode and began to learn interior prayer in the way I had been shown, and to go to see my *starets* (spiritual advisor or elder) from time to time.

For a week, alone in my garden, I steadily set myself to learn to pray without ceasing exactly as the *starets* had explained. At first things seemed to go very well. But it tired me very much. I felt lazy and bored and overwhelmingly sleepy, and a cloud of all sorts of other things closed round me. I went in distress to my *starets* and told him the state I was in.

He greeted me in a friendly way and turned to the teaching of Nicephorus and read, "If after a few attempts you do not succeed in reaching the realm of your heart in the way you have been taught, do what I am about to say, and by God's help you will find what you seek. The faculty of pronouncing words lies in the throat. Reject all other thoughts (you can do this if you will) and allow that faculty to repeat only the following words constantly, 'Lord Jesus Christ, have mercy on me.' Compel yourself to do it always. If you succeed for a time, then without a doubt you also will open to prayer. We know it from experience."

"There you have the teaching of the holy Fathers on cases," said my *starets,* "and therefore you ought from today onwards to carry but my directions with confidence, and repeat the Prayer of Jesus as often as possible. Here is a rosary. Take it, and to start with, *say the Prayer three thousand times a day*. Whether you are standing or sitting, walking or lying down, continually repeat 'Lord Jesus Christ, have mercy on me.' Say it quietly and without hurry, but without fail exactly three thousand times a day without deliberately increasing or diminishing the number. God will help you and by this means you will reach also the unceasing activity of the heart."

I gladly accepted this guidance and went home and began to carry out faithfully and exactly what my *starets* had bidden. For two days I found it rather difficult, but after that it became so easy and likeable, that as soon as I stopped, I felt a sort of need to go on saying the Prayer of Jesus, and I did it freely and willingly, not forcing myself to it as before.

I reported to my *starets,* and he bade me *say the Prayer six thousand times a day,* saying, "be calm, just try as faithfully as possible to carry out the set number of prayers. God will vouchsafe you His grace."

In my lonely hut I said the Prayer of Jesus six thousand times a day for a whole week. I felt no anxiety. Taking no notice of any other thoughts however much they assailed me, I had but one object, i.e., to carry out my *starets'* bidding exactly. And what happened? I grew so used to my Prayer that when I stopped for a single moment, I felt, so to speak, as though something were missing, as though I had lost something. The very moment I started the Prayer again, it went on easily and joyously. If I met anyone I had no wish to talk to him. All I wanted was to be alone and to say my Prayer, so used to it had I become in a week.

My *starets* had not seen me for ten days. On the eleventh day he came to see me himself, and I told him how things were going. He listened and said, "Now you have got used to the Prayer. See that you preserve the habit and strengthen it. Waste no time, therefore, but make up your mind by God's help from today to *say the Prayer of Jesus twelve thousand times a day*. Remain in your solitude, get up early, go to bed late, and come and ask advice of me every fortnight."

I did as he bade me. The first day I scarcely succeeded in finishing my task of saying twelve thousand prayers by late evening. The second day I did it easily and contentedly. To begin with, this ceaseless saying of the prayer brought a certain amount of weariness, my tongue felt numbed, I had a stiff sort of feeling in my jaws, I had a feeling at first pleasant but afterwards lightly painful in the roof of my mouth. The thumb of my left hand, with which I counted my beads, hurt a little. I felt a slight inflammation in the whole of that wrist, and even up to the elbow, which was not unpleasant. Moreover, all this aroused me, as it were, and urged me on to frequent saying of the Prayer. For five days I did my set number of twelve thousand and as I formed the habit I found at the same time pleasure and satisfaction in it.

Early one morning, the Prayer woke me up as it were. I started to say my usual morning prayers, but my tongue

> THE RUSSIAN PILGRIM PRAYED THE JESUS PRAYER: "LORD JESUS CHRIST, HAVE MERCY ON ME" TWELVE THOUSAND TIMES A DAY FOR THE LENGTH OF A SUMMER.

refused to say them easily or exactly. My whole desire was fixed upon one thing only—to say the Prayer of Jesus, and as soon as I went on with it I was filled with joy and relief. It was as though my lips and my tongue pronounced the words entirely of themselves without any urging from me. I spent the whole day in a state of the greatest contentment; I felt as though I was cut off from everything else. I lived as though in another world, and I easily finished my twelve thousand prayers by the early evening. I felt very much like still going on with them, but I did not dare to go beyond the number my starets had set me. Every day following I went on in the same way with my calling on the Name of Jesus Christ, and that with great readiness and liking. Then I went to see my *starets* and told him everything frankly and in detail.

He heard me out and then said, "Now I give you my permission to say your Prayer as often as you wish and as often as you can. Try to devote every moment you are awake to the Prayer, call on the Name of Jesus Christ without counting the number of times, and submit yourself humbly to the will of God, looking to Him for help. I am sure He will not forsake you, and that He will lead you into the right path."

Under this guidance I spent the whole summer in *ceaseless oral prayer* to Jesus Christ, and I felt absolute peace in my soul. During sleep I often dreamed that I was saying the Prayer. And during the day if I happened to meet anyone, all men without exception were as dear to me as if they had been my nearest relations. But I did not concern myself with them much. All my ideas were quite calmed of their own accord. I thought of nothing whatever but my Prayer, my mind tended to listen to it, and my heart began of itself to feel at times a certain warmth and pleasure. If I happened to go to church, the lengthy service of the monastery seemed short to me and no longer wearied me as it had in time past. My lonely hut seemed like a splendid palace, and I knew not how to thank God for having sent to me, a lost sinner, so wholesome a guide and master. . . .

And this is how I go about now, and ceaselessly repeat the Prayer of Jesus, which is more precious and sweet to me than anything in the world. At times I do as much as forty-three or four miles a day, and do not feel I am walking at all. I am aware only of the fact that I am saying my Prayer. When the bitter cold pierces me, I begin to say my Prayer more earnestly and I quickly get warm all over. When hunger begins to overcome me, I call more often on the Name of Jesus, and I forget my wish for food. When I fall ill and get rheumatism in my back and legs, I fix my thoughts on the Prayer and do not notice the pain. If anyone harms me I have only to think, "How sweet is the Prayer of Jesus!" and the injury and the anger alike pass away and I forget it all. I have no cares and no interests. The fussy business of the world I would not give a glance to. The one thing I wish for is to be alone and all by myself to pray, to pray without ceasing; and doing this, I am filled with joy. God knows what is happening to me! Of course, all this is sensuous, or as my departed *starets* said, an artificial state which follows naturally upon routine. But because of my unworthiness and stupidity I dare not venture yet to go on further, and learn and make my own spiritual prayer within the depths of my heart. I await God's time. And in the meanwhile I rest my hope on the prayers of my departed *starets,* thus, although I have not yet reached that ceaseless spiritual prayer which is self-acting in the heart, yet I thank God I do now understand the meaning of those words I heard in the Epistle—"Pray without ceasing."[2]

To many of us at the end of the twentieth century, this may seem like a somewhat strange and bizarre experience—a lonely peasant, sitting in a little hut or walking many miles a day, reciting the same Jesus prayer 12,000 times a day. However, his own testimony shows that he attained the very thing we desire—to be filled in the constant presence of God. Contrast that to our modern approach, where we come to the throne of God quite casually—at times even sleepily—confident that our loving heavenly Father accepts our indifference. But as we begin to do some serious business with God and pursue Him with all of our heart, we find, as the pilgrim did, that focused prayer must replace casual prayer. It is not necessarily the recitation of a particular phrase or the method of prayer that is of importance, but the degree of desire and focus that propels us into the pursuit of His presence.

In the story of the pilgrim above, a great degree of desire for God's presence was evident. Another man with an equally intense desire was Brother Lawrence. His method of contemplation, although slightly different from the pilgrim's way, yielded similar results. Brother Lawrence started his search for the ceaseless presence of God with an intense life of vocal prayer. For some reason, this attempt to push forward led him to many self-doubts and guilt over his own sinfulness and unworthiness. He was engulfed in 10 years of intense anxiety in which he even doubted his own salvation.[3] But Brother Lawrence continued to pray and continued to push on. Finally, in desperation, he cried out to God and said, "It no longer matters to me what I do or what I suffer, provided that I remain lovingly united to Your will."[4] His story continues:

> In a moment, God opened Brother Lawrence's eyes. He received a divine revelation of God's majesty that illuminated his Spirit. . . . From that moment, meditating on the character and lovingkindness of God molded Brother Lawrence's character. It became so natural to him that he passed the next forty years of his life in the continuous practice of the presence of God, which he described as a quiet, familiar conversation with Him.[5]

BROTHER LAWRENCE PASSED THE NEXT FORTY YEARS OF HIS LIFE IN THE CONTINUOUS PRACTICE OF THE PRESENCE OF GOD, WHICH HE DESCRIBED AS A QUIET, FAMILIAR CONVERSATION WITH HIM.

Brother Lawrence gives several keys as to why he was able to cultivate a deep presence of God in his heart. He eventually moved from vocal prayer to nonverbal prayer that "was maintained by the heart and by love, rather than by understanding and speech."[6] Therefore, the only words necessary were "short phrases . . . inspired by love."[7] He said that he reached a state that "even if [he was] reading the Word or praying out loud, [he would] stop for a few minutes—as often as possible—to praise God from the depths of [his] heart, to enjoy Him there in secret."[8] He soon "began to live as if there were no one else but God and [him]self in the world."[9] He said, "I often held my Spirit in His holy presence, recalling it whenever it went astray."[10]

He also said that "his prayers consisted totally and simply of God's presence. Thus, when he was not in prayer, he felt practically the same way as when he was in prayer."[11] To his dying breath, Brother Lawrence exhorted his fellow brothers "to believe him, and count for lost all the time that is not spent in loving God."[12]

As Brother Lawrence's story elucidates, growth in our prayer life cannot help but lead us to an ever-deepening intimacy with God. Therefore, if we persevere in prayer, we will one day— maybe even somewhat unconsciously, without knowing where it began or how it happened—find ourselves moving from vocal prayer to silent contemplation. One becomes the prerequisite for the other.

HOW DOES ONE DISCOVER THE PRAYER OF CONTEMPLATION?

Again that doctor of the Church, Saint Teresa of Avila, taught her followers to say vocal prayer as a precondition to silent contemplation. She would tell her nuns that "while you are repeating the

Paternoster (the Our Father), or some other vocal prayer, it is quite possible for the Lord to grant you perfect contemplation."[13] She fully believed that saying prayers out loud first was the route to silent contemplation:

> I know there are many persons who while praying vocally are raised by God to sublime contemplation. . . . It's because of this that I insist so much, daughters, upon your reciting vocal prayer well.[14]

MEDITATION

So we see that the eventual response of meditation (which is spoken or muttered) is contemplation (which is unspoken). By its very nature, contemplative prayer is silent prayer. At the deeper levels of prayer, there comes a point when words do get in the way. As one philosopher put it:

> The purpose of words is to convey ideas. When ideas are grasped, the words are forgotten. Where can I find a man who has forgotten words? He is the one I would like to talk to.[15]

Therefore, it simply follows that after one learns how to vocalize prayer by praying the Scriptures

THE PURPOSE OF WORDS IS TO CONVEY IDEAS. WHEN IDEAS ARE GRASPED, THE WORDS ARE FORGOTTEN. WHERE CAN I FIND A MAN WHO HAS FORGOTTEN WORDS? HE IS THE ONE I WOULD LIKE TO TALK TO.

out loud to God, one begins to enter into a much deeper concentration on the Person of God. This is because the purpose of the *words* of the Bible is to lead us to the *author* of those words. Inevitably, meditation on the Scriptures will cause us to understand something of the mind and heart of the One who writes them. The words take us to the Person, and silence then replaces words, taking us to depths that words cannot plumb. Prayer has now become a wordless exchange of affection and love. One loves and is loved. At this deeper level, words actually inhibit, rather than increase, the communion that is taking place. Prayer has now become a communication of feelings and spirit rather than words and ideas. Yet, this type of prayer is a natural outgrowth of focused verbal meditation. It usually happens imperceptibly as the Lord responds to our petitions.

> Infused contemplation is the normal, ordinary development of discursive (i.e., vocal) prayer. **The former gradually replaces the latter when reasoned thought has run its course as a method of communing with the Lord.** Infused prayer is given, not produced. Unlike oriental states of awareness, our prayer is **a love communion** that the divine Beloved Himself gives when we are ready for it. . . . The prayer cannot be "figured out" or understood. Trying to analyze it by clear, concise ideas or concepts not only issues in frustration, but also indicates a lack of understanding of what contemplation is.[16]

SILENCE

We need to underscore this point. Silence in prayer is often not something we orchestrate; rather, it is a gift that can come upon us quite unexpectedly. Instead of rushing to fill the gap, we learn to embrace the gift as the better part of our time of prayer.

From time to time you will begin to touch the state of inward silence. What shall be your response to such an experience? One thing is this: No longer burden yourself with spoken prayer. (At this time, to pray out loud, or in any conventional way, would only draw you away from an inward experience and draw you back to an outward surface prayer.) But if you do not speak, what shall you do? Nothing! Simply yield to the inward drawing! Yield to the wooing of your spirit. Your spirit is drawing you deeper within.[17]

In silence, God has a bed for His revelation to rest on. For this reason, Scripture is filled with exhortations to silence. One of the most memorable of these is found in Psalm 46:10: "*Be still,* and know that I am God" (emphasis added). Dare we think about the corollary to this—that if we are not still, we may never truly know that God is God? Psalm 4:4 (*KJV*) exclaims: "Stand in awe, and sin not: commune with your own heart upon your bed, and be still." Exodus 14:14 (*NASB*) offers another encouraging reason for silence: "The LORD will fight for you while you keep silent."

Jeanne Guyon, expands on this idea:

You and I are very weak. If you, in your weakness, attempt to attack your enemies, you will often find yourself wounded. There is another way. In times of temptation and distraction, remain by faith in the simple presence of Jesus Christ. You will find an immediate supply of strength. . . . [The silence of turning to God is] the highest activity the soul can engage in: total dependence on the Spirit of God. This should always be your main concern.[18]

Throughout the ages, many devout saints have described this point in prayer where words are no longer necessary. As we are bombarded by sound in our modern world, this can sometimes be difficult for us to imagine. Many of us have experienced the discomfort of silence; perhaps fewer have enjoyed its comfort. As quoted earlier:

The purpose of the word is to convey ideas. When ideas are grasped, the words are forgotten. Where can I find a man who has forgotten words? He is the one I would like to talk to.[19]

Think back to the reason you began to pray in the first place. Whatever that reason was, it was most certainly not just to generate a certain number of words for a certain time each day. You have a serious purpose in praying. What we are really after is the ability to live out the first commandment, namely, to love the God who loved us first, with all the passion and strength we possess. Therefore, words become unnecessary when their purpose has been fulfilled. Words take us to a pinnacle of silence where God's manifest presence speaks without words. At this point, the silence of communion with God becomes a delight for both parties. However, the discipline of silence may take more practice than any other for us. Henri

Nouwen comments that we have become so contaminated by our wordy world that we hold to the deceptive opinion that our words are more important than our silence.[20]

In silent contemplation, a supernatural drawing occurs. Having come to the end of words, we simply stare in silence at the Person of God. One of the most apt, and most beautiful, descriptions of the essence of contemplation that I have heard comes from a simple farmer:

> [Think of the] wonderful description given by that unlettered farm-labourer at Ars who used to remain for hours in stillness and silence gazing at the tabernacle, and when the Cure d'Ars asked him what he did there, he simply replied: "I look at him, and he looks at me."[21]

The words fade and His face grows. One begins to feel like David did in wanting the "one thing"—communion with God—more than all else:

> *One thing* I have asked from the LORD, that I shall seek: that I may dwell in the house of the LORD all the days of my life, *to behold the beauty of the LORD,* and *to meditate in His temple* (Ps. 27:4, *NASB*, emphasis added).

COMMUNION

The reality is that even though the communion may be wordless, or perhaps with only simple repetition of one or two words, the understanding is profoundly moved. At the deepest interpersonal level possible, an interchange of love is occurring. And although contemplation usually starts with a person pouring out his or her emotions *for* God, often one is swept up into a realm where one is overtaken by love *from* God. At such moments, it is hard to distinguish where the human spirit ends and the divine starts. To the outside observer, it might look like the description given by Saint Francis's companion, Bernard, who tells the story of Saint Francis caught up in contemplation:

> With face turned to heaven, and hands and eyes lifted to God, in complete surrender and with the warmest devotion, he prayed, saying: "My God, my All." These words he groaned out to God, with copious tears, again and again with solemn devotion until dawn: "My God, my All"—and no more.[22]

This is a good illustration of the external simplicity and the obvious internal profundity in the practice of contemplation. Saint Francis prayed four mere words, but they led him to be overtaken by the presence of God for hours on end. One of the Desert Fathers, John Climacus, expounded this point when he said:

> When you find satisfaction or compunction in a certain word of your prayer, stop at that point.[23]

Saint Teresa has a similar prescription for attaining depth in contemplation. Once, when a nun asked her how to become contemplative, she paused for a moment and then answered, "Sister, you know how to say the 'Our Father,' don't you? Well, just take an hour to do it!"[24]

HOW DOES ONE ENTER THE PRAYER OF CONTEMPLATION?

Since contemplation is basically a love exchange between a person and God, one enters the realm of contemplation by shutting out all external activity and reminding oneself of the Cross—where God's love was most greatly manifested. Usually I try to recall an image of God as He has appeared to me in a vision, or in other images and metaphors where He has revealed Himself in Scripture. (Perhaps this is where the tradition of iconography began.) Then, I try to hold my spirit in silence before the Lord and worship by pouring out my love on an aspect of His beauty. Generally, this focus on aspects of His Personhood produces a spiritual connection. One actually feels his or her spirit connect on an affective level with the Spirit of God. A mutual interchange of love occurs.

PERSONAL EXAMPLE

In order to elucidate this abstract concept better, I will try to explain with a concrete example. Recently, I was meditating on the description of Jesus Christ in Revelation 1:12-14 (*NASB*):

> And I turned to see the voice that was speaking with me. And having turned I saw seven golden lampstands; and in the middle of the lampstands one like a son of man, clothed in a robe reaching to the feet, and girded across His breast with a golden girdle. And His head and His hair were white like white wool, like snow; and His eyes were like a flame of fire.

As I began to concentrate on His head and His hair, I began to cry. The very description of His head and His hair touched me with the understanding of His incredible purity. John saw the brilliant whiteness, and it is as though he can't say how white it was. It was white—like white wool, like snow. And His whole head is white, not just His hair. The interior response of my soul was to worship His holiness and His purity while at the same time being very aware of my own impurity. I began to weep because of the attraction of how perfect He is. My emotions were overwhelmed with deep gratitude that His blood has washed me from my sins. I had an innate knowledge of how far I am from being holy, and this caused me to weep more. Like Isaiah who saw the Lord, I said, "I am a man of unclean lips, and I live among a people of unclean lips" (Isa. 6:5).

Rather than feeling shame, however, a flood of worship filled my heart for the very purity that is Him. I was over-whelmed with thankfulness that, in spite of the corruption that exists everywhere in the world, there is One who is completely holy. A feeling of security and safety came to me because of this purity, and I was drawn deeper into who He is through it. There is safety in His holiness. I was filled with love for Him, because He is utterly pure. An earnest longing to be closer to Him and to become like Him overcame me. I just kept thinking of how much I love Him for who He is. There is no one like Him.

Then without trying, my mind raced to other descriptions of Him. I thought of the Scripture where Daniel described the Ancient of Days as having white hair (see Dan. 7:9). To think that He has always been holy, always been pure—from ancient times—brought more worship. The fact that He was standing "in the middle of the lampstands" was yet more cause for worship.

There is this perfectly pure One, and He is so close to us—in the middle of His churches—so holy and so close. The more I contemplated Him, the more I loved Him for how He can be who He is and still be so close to me.

But this description of contemplation would not be complete without saying that while all of these understandings were going through my head (since it all happened in silence), I also felt that I was the recipient of this pure love. I was thinking about Him, yet I was feeling touched by Him. I actually felt pure love going into me the whole while I was thinking about Him. The words of Bob Birch, an aged intercessor for the Canadian Church, rang true: "Heart to heart, spirit to Spirit, as the virgin Bride, we seek His face." That's what it is—it is "heart to heart" and "spirit to Spirit." This is the prayer of silence. It is communion. It is "an immersion in God, an absorption in the Beloved."[25]

PRACTICAL EXAMPLE

I would like to give a practical example of how you might begin the prayer of contemplation. As with all prayer, we start by talking to God, but with contemplation, we begin by meditating on a specific aspect of God's nature. Generally, it is good to find a scriptural passage that delineates one such aspect. I would encourage you to start with a very small selection of Scripture— one verse is usually more than enough. For example, Exodus 34:6-7 is loaded with divine attributes. (It could take weeks to get through just these two verses!) It is in this passage that God describes to Moses specifically what His glory is:

> Then the LORD passed by in front of him and proclaimed,
> "The LORD, the LORD God, compassionate and gracious,

slow to anger, and abounding in lovingkindness and truth; who keeps lovingkindness for thousands, who forgives iniquity, transgression and sin; yet He will by no means leave the guilty unpunished, visiting the iniquity of fathers on the children and on the grandchildren to the third and fourth generations" (Exod. 34:6-7, *NASB*).

You may choose to start by repeating slowly, "The Lord, the Lord God" as you direct your focus to Him. "The Lord, the Lord God." As you do this, position yourself before Him. Picture Him in your mind's eye (i.e., on His throne as in Revelation 4). As your heart and mind attain focused concentration, go to the next word—"compassionate"—and begin to worship Him for all of His compassion. Often you will be reminded of other biblical passages on the subject of compassion. Worship Him silently with those passages as they come to mind. *I thank You, Lord, for Your compassion. You are full of compassion and mercy* (see Jas. 5:11). *It is Your glory. You are the compassionate God.* With every image that arises on the subject of compassion, turn it into praise and worship. You may visualize Jesus healing crowds of sick people; thus, meditate on the motivation of His heart while He healed them. "When Jesus landed and saw a large crowd, he had compassion on them and healed their sick" (Matt. 14:14).

You will soon begin to see how different His motivations are from ours. Just looking at a large crowd moved Him to compassion. Meditate on His glory that does kind acts out of pure compassion. He is the Father of compassion (see 2 Cor. 1:3) whose compassion is great (see Ps. 119:156) and deep (see Isa. 54:7). Your praise of Him is, of course, inaudible, with only a few words repeated, such as "the Lord, the Lord God" or "compassionate One." Do not try to become theological at this point, but continue gazing into who He is. It is God alone—God the Father, God the Son and God the Holy Spirit—the originator of compassion. Worship this attribute of His glory silently and repeatedly, as long as you feel His anointing on it. Then move on to the next attribute, and begin again to worship Him for the glory of His grace. Sometimes the Lord will come upon you in your time of silent worship, overwhelming you with other understandings of this attribute. These understandings may be applied personally or corporately, but the revelation of His beauty in them always causes us to love Him.

In contemplation, "God slakes the soul's thirst and feeds its hunger."[26] God gives the meditator a new wine and lifts him or her above the normal meditative self into the sphere of experienced transcendence. Here at last is an infused element of prayer. Here the Spirit prays in the human spirit. One experiences a state of inner harmony; carnal motions are quieted; the flesh is not at odds with the spirit; the person is in a state of spiritual integration. The light of God's presence shines through the soul experientially. The love of God is no longer abstract but concretely poured into the receiving self. One can see oneself being loved and loving in return. Clearly, we are speaking of a pure gift at this point. These moments can be fleeting or prolonged, subtle or pronounced. They can go and come again. They can mingle with the flow of meditative words repeated, thoughts reflected, intuitions enjoyed or resolutions enacted. But the person is more still and passive; our God is passing by.

Incidentally, we must leave room for individuation in contemplation. It will look similar but not exactly the same, for different people. After all, God made each one of us unique and, therefore, has a unique relationship with each one of us. He loves us as His corporate Bride and as individuals. However you enter the prayer of silence, however you develop the art of looking at Him, be assured that at the end of your silence, you will find Him. It's His promise.

> *"You will seek me and find me when you seek me with all your heart.*
> *I will be found by you," declares the LORD.*
>
> JEREMIAH 29:13-14

CONCLUSION

After Jesus finished His three years of ministry and was about to return to heaven, He called the 11 disciples to Him and commissioned them, saying:

> All authority in heaven and on earth has been given to me. Therefore go and make disciples of all nations (Matt. 28:18-19).

Authority had been given to Jesus, and He was now delegating it to His disciples. He was sending them out as ambassadors to make disciples of all the *ethnee* (which is Greek for "tribe"), or tribes, groups, peoples and nations. For our part, we believe that the primary means of discipleship is prayer. As mentioned earlier, it is the means that the Muslims have used to disciple a sixth of the earth (over 1.3 billion Muslims). It is also one of the main ways that Yahweh used to teach His people—Israel. Furthermore, Jesus told His disciples to teach the ethnee to obey, that is, to do what He commanded His disciples to do. At the top of Jesus' priority list, He taught and led people toward loving God the Father, which was facilitated through the practice of prayer.

PLAY A ROLE IN THE GREAT COMMISSION

It's important to remember that if you are not growing in the practice of prayer yourself and then teaching others to pray, you are missing a huge part of the Great Commission. We would like everyone to make it their life's goal to become a lover of God, evidenced and fueled by praying the Bible out loud to Him every day. But don't stop there. You can then disciple others to do the same. We labor to see the vision statement of PRAYING THE BIBLE INTERNATIONAL become a reality, namely, that *a billion people begin to pray the Bible out loud to God every day!*

> OUR VISION STATEMENT IS THAT *A BILLION PEOPLE BEGIN TO PRAY THE BIBLE OUT LOUD TO GOD EVERY DAY!*

We don't believe that it's acceptable that more than 1 billion Muslims bow down every day and chant Koranic scriptures out loud to a god who is not God, while a third of the earth—those who espouse some sort of allegiance to

Jesus Christ and the people to whom the command was origi-nally given—hardly pray at all. We believe that it is God's will that a minimum of a tithe of the earth join the angels in daily, heart-felt praise, saying with a loud voice:

> Worthy is the Lamb, who was slain, to receive *power* and *wealth* and *wisdom* and *strength* and *honor* and *glory* and *praise!* (Rev. 5:12, emphasis added).

We at PRAYING THE BIBLE INTERNATIONAL believe it's time that the devil does not get his way because of the sheer neg-lect of over a billion believers who presently do not first of all pray for kings and those in authority so that they may lead quiet and peaceable lives (see 2 Tim. 1:1-8). It's time we were provoked by the example of a billion Muslims praying out loud to Allah five times a day. It's time the earth changed!

However, this sort of thing does not just happen because it is a good idea or merely because we want it to. A billion people is a substantial section of the whole of Christendom. For a change in heart to occur, it will take anointing, massive work and a con-certed, focused effort. It will take everyone praying themselves and discipling everyone they can to pray the Bible. Take heart—the One who leads this Great Commission is a fiery intercessor Himself. He is the glorious Man, Christ Jesus.

Disciple Yourself in Praying the Bible

What can you do? Disciple yourself and your family in praying the Bible out loud to God every day. Let us hear from you. E-mail us and tell us who you are, where you live and with whom you fellowship. Tell us your story of how and what praying the Bible has done for you. Was it hard getting started? Did you experience some amazing prayer answers from God? What do other people say about it? Have you been getting your children to pray the Bible? Check out our website and hear other stories from people who are praying the Bible, and get your children to participate in the Praying the Bible Club at www.prayingthebible.com.

> WE ARE LOOKING FOR TENS OF THOUSANDS OF PEOPLE TO BECOME PRAYING THE BIBLE PRESENTERS, WHO WILL EVANGELIZE OTHERS TO PRAY THE BIBLE OUT LOUD TO GOD EVERY DAY.

BECOME A PRAYING THE BIBLE PRESENTER

We are looking for tens of thousands of people to become Praying the Bible presenters, who will teach this message to their Sunday School or small group, or preach this message to their entire congregation. We are looking to cooperate with all denomination leaders to help them facilitate this word into their sphere of influence. We want to connect with all parachurch agencies (especially prayer ministries) who are interested in praying the Bible. We want to show them how it can help their vision. We also want to equip conference speakers who will carry this message into their conferences and seminars. Finally, we are looking for entrepreneurs who are interested in creatively partnering together to help finance the spread of this message—particularly in the more difficult areas of the poorer nations of the world. We want to impact every sector of Christendom in every geographical region of every people group of the world, namely:

1. Roman Catholic
2. Orthodox
3. Coptic
4. Mainline Protestant
5. Evangelical
6. Pentecostal/Charismatic
7. New Apostolic Reformation Churches

E-mail us at info@prayingthebible.com to request a free copy of our outlines for overheads or PowerPoint/media presentations. These are available in one-, three- or five-hour segments. We will provide complete study notes and presentation tips. In addition, videos, audiocassettes, CDs and a host of other resources are available to help you disciple those around you in the greatest experience of their life—praying the Bible.

SPREAD THE MESSAGE

Who do you know? Do you know a way that the praying the Bible message can reach more people? Who do you think would benefit from this message or would like this message to impact their circle of influence? We will help to facilitate this message getting to your area and even make the resources available to you. Pass on to your friends the essence of the praying the Bible message by way of an e-mail article available on request at info@prayingthebible.com or on our website at www.prayingth ebible.com.

GET THE PRAYING THE BIBLE RESOURCES INTO YOUR CHURCH AND CITY

Praying the Bible International will help you obtain all of the prayer resources you need for your prayer group, church or movement, including books, CDs and audiocassettes at distribution wholesale rates. If your Christian bookstore does not have these resources, we will help you get them into your city. Our goal is to spread the message far and wide and to disciple the world in making this happen. Refer to the back pages for a list of our resources.

PRAY!

Paul said, "Finally, brothers, pray for us that the message of the Lord may spread rapidly and be honored, just as it was with you" (2 Thess. 3:1). We all need to continue to pray for the worldwide prayer movement. In the last few decades, the maturity that the Church has gained in prayer has been more than in any other time in history. Pray that more and more people will understand and practice daily prayer, especially praying the Bible every day. Pray for open doors—that this one unique message will take root in every church and Christian family in the world. Let's believe God to see the glory of the Lord cover the earth as the waters cover the sea in these great times in which we live.

Amen, come Lord Jesus.

APPENDIX A

ORGANIZATION "PRAYING THE BIBLE" PRAYER CHART

We have included this chart to help you get in the habit of praying the Bible. There is an important philosophy behind it. We have found that everybody needs structure and that good habits are formed through repetition and consistency. For centuries, the people of God engaged in the regular routine of praying the Bible. When you form the habit, the habit forms you.

Children, in particular, need to be taught to pray. In working with our own children for over three years, we have discovered that unless something is in place children can easily follow, the practice dissipates. A daily chart, which they can fill out and bring to you, will not only help them form a habit, it will also put the onus on them to get it done. While it makes prayer time fun, it also forms a good habit. Younger children will benefit greatly by getting it signed by a parent every day.

We also want to underscore the idea of privilege versus punishment. The intention is not to punish children for not saying their prayers. Yet it is very biblical to withhold privileges. In our household, the way it works is: "Pray today, play tomorrow. No pray? No play!" If they forget to pray, they lose a privilege; however, when they have filled out a chart, we reward them. Children like rewards.

The chart is fairly self-explanatory. All you need to do is photocopy it, insert the dates, check off which section of prayers has been prayed and write down the specific verses of text. Adults and children alike can use the chart to regain the lost art of daily prayers.

Organizational "Praying the Bible" Prayer Chart

Name: _____

Week of: _____

W E E K D A Y S			
	MONDAY	TUESDAY	WEDNESDAY
Prayer Categories	Today I prayed...	Today I prayed...	Today I prayed...
	☑ Text	☑ Text	☑ Text
Theophanies	❏	❏	❏
Psalms	❏	❏	❏
Wisdom	❏	❏	❏
Songs	❏	❏	❏
Prophets	❏	❏	❏
Jesus	❏	❏	❏
Apostolic	❏	❏	❏
Hymns	❏	❏	❏
Extra Prayers	❏	❏	❏
Prayed # Min.	min.	min.	min.
Today I felt...			

WEEKDAYS			
THURSDAY	*FRIDAY*	*SATURDAY*	*SUNDAY*
Today I prayed...	*Today I prayed...*	*Today I prayed...*	*Today I prayed...*
☑ Text	☑ Text	☑ Text	☑ Text
❏	❏	❏	❏
❏	❏	❏	❏
❏	❏	❏	❏
❏	❏	❏	❏
❏	❏	❏	❏
❏	❏	❏	❏
❏	❏	❏	❏
❏	❏	❏	❏
❏	❏	❏	❏
min.	*min.*	*min.*	*min.*

APPENDIX B

88 BIBLE PRAYERS FROM *PRAYING THE BIBLE: THE BOOK OF PRAYERS*

THEOPHANIES

Visions of God
Ezekiel 1:1-28

Yahweh and the Ten Commandments
Exodus 19:16-20,24-25; 20:1-21

Show Me Your Glory
Exodus 33:15-19; 34:5-8,29

Eyes and Wings
Ezekiel 10:1-22

Here I Am, Send Me
Isaiah 6:1-8

The Ancient of Days
Daniel 7:9-10,13-14,18,21-22,24-27

The Heavenly Man in Linen
Daniel 10:1—11:1; 12:8-10

The Glorified Son of Man
Revelation 1:9-18

The Heavenly Throne Room
Revelation 4:1-11

Faithful and True
Revelation 19:11-16

THE PSALMS

Blessed Is the Man
Psalm 1:1-6

Fearfully and Wonderfully Made
Psalm 139:1-24

A Prayer of Repentance
Psalm 51:1-19

Save Me, O God
Psalm 16:1-11

The Lord Is My Shepherd
Psalm 23

Battle Hymn of the King
Psalm 18:1-14,16-29,31-43,46,49-50

Under the Shadow of His Wings
Psalm 91

Better Is One Day
Psalm 84

Jesus' Prayer from the Cross
Psalm 22

Lift Up Your Heads
Psalm 24

A Prayer for Leaders
Psalm 20

A Blessing Psalm of Ascents
Psalm 128

PRAYERS OF WISDOM

A Time for Everything
Ecclesiastes 3:1-8,11

Wisdom Calls Out
*Proverbs 2:1-6; 9:10-11; 7:4;
23:12; 4:7*

The Righteous Workman
*Proverbs 24:30-34; 23:4; 14:23;
10:4-5; 26:13-14; 18:9; 22:29*

Let My Words Be Few
*Psalm 39:1; Proverbs 13:3; 18:21;
12:18; 10:19; 15:1; 20:3; 12:16; 25:15;
Ecclesiastes 5:2*

Deliver Me from Evil
*Job 31:1; Proverbs 6:24-27,29; 30:20;
6:32-33; 2:18-19; 5:15,18-19,21*

Mercy
*Proverbs 14:31; 22:2,22-23; 29:7;
19:17; Job 29:12-13,15-17,25*

Virtue and Honor
*Proverbs 4:20,22-23; 21:21; 4:24,26;
22:1; 3:9-10; 13:20; 1 Corinthians
15:33; Proverbs 10:27*

The Way of a King
*Proverbs 30:29-31; 25:2; 8:15-16;
Ecclesiastes 4:13; Proverbs 29:4,14;
31:2-5,8*

In Praise of the Noble Wife
Proverbs 31:10-12,14-18,20,23,25-31

The Whole Duty of Man
Ecclesiastes 12:1-7,13-14

THE SONG OF SONGS

**Beginnings of Intimacy and
Revelation**
Song of Songs 1:2-7

Faint with Love
Song of Songs 1:15—2:7

**Embracing the Lover's
Coming**
Song of Songs 2:8-17

The Dark Night of Love
Song of Songs 3:1-5

The Might of the Lover
Song of Songs 3:6-11

The Beauty of the Beloved
Song of Songs 4:7-12,15-16

Anticipation
Song of Songs 5:2-8

Altogether Lovely
Song of Songs 5:9-16

The Ravished Bridegroom
Song of Songs 6:4-10,13

The Outpouring of
Divine Love
Ephesians 3:14-21

The Release of Prophetic
Boldness
Ephesians 6:18-20

Overflowing Holy Love
Philippians 1:3-4,9-11

Filled with a Knowledge of
His Will
Colossians 1:2-4,9-12

The Door of God
Colossians 4:2-4,12

The Established Heart
1 Thessalonians 3:9-13; 5:23-25

Fulfill Your Call
2 Thessalonians 1:3,11-12

Increase Your Word
2 Thessalonians 3:1-3,5,16

Just Say No!
Titus 2:11-13

A Prayer of Prosperity
3 John 1:2

Jude's Doxology
Jude 1:24-25

The Apostolic Benediction
2 Corinthians 13:11-14

HYMNS OF THE REVELATION

Look . . . He Is Coming!
Revelation 1:4-7

The Overcomer's Prayer
*Revelation 2:1,7-8,11-12,17-18,26-29;
3:1,5-7,12-14,21-22*

Holy, Holy, Holy!
Revelation 4:8-11

Worthy Is the Lamb
Revelation 5:8-14

The Martyr's Cry
Revelation 6:9-11

Praise of the End-Time
Harvest
Revelation 7:9-17

Time to Reign
Revelation 11:15-18

Overcoming the Dragon
Revelation 12:7-12

The Song of Moses
Revelation 15:2-4

Just and True
Revelation 16:1,5-7

The Wedding Song
Revelation 19:1-8

Come, Lord Jesus!
Revelation 22:12-17,20

APPENDIX C

EIGHTEEN BENEDICTIONS OF JEWISH PRAYERS

My Lord, open my lips, and I will tell your praise.

1. Blessed are you, Lord, our God and the God of our forefathers, God of Abraham, God of Isaac and God of Jacob. The God, the Great, the Powerful, the Awesome, Most High God who does good deeds of loving-kindness and is the Creator of everything and remembers the deeds of loving-kindness of our forefathers, and who brings a redeemer to their children's children, for the sake of His name, with love. King, Helper, Savior and Shield. Blessed are You, God, Shield of Abraham.

2. You are great forever, my Lord; You revive the dead, with great salvation. You cause the wind to blow and the rain to fall. You nourish the living with loving-kindness; you revive the dead with great compassion, support the falling and heal the sick, and release the imprisoned, and fulfill Your faithfulness to those who sleep in the dust. Who is like You, Master of Strength, who can be compared to You? You are a King who causes death, [for purpose of] bringing the person

back to life. Blessed are You, God, who resurrects the dead. (The reader may say the Kedusha here.)

3. You are Holy, and Your Name is Holy, and the holy ones praise you everyday, forever. Blessed are You, God, the Holy God.

4. You graciously give man discerning knowledge and teach people understanding. Graciously grant us from Yourself discerning knowledge, understanding and intellect. Blessed are You, God, who graciously grants discerning knowledge.

5. Return us, our Father, to Your Torah, and bring us close, our King, to Your service, and return us with complete repentance before You. Blessed are You, God, who desires repentance.

6. Forgive us, our Father, for we have sinned unintentionally. Pardon us, our King, for we have purposely sinned, for You pardon and forgive. Blessed are You, God, the gracious One who forgives abundantly.

7. Please look at our affliction, and fight our battles, and redeem us quickly for Your name's sake because You are a mighty Redeemer. Blessed are You, God, Redeemer of Israel.

8. Heal us, Lord, and we will be healed. Save us, and we will be saved, since our praise is to You. And bring

about a complete remedy for all of our afflictions, for You are God, a King who is a faithful and compassionate healer. Blessed are You, God, who heals the sick of His people, Israel.

9. Bless upon us, Lord, our God, this year and all of its types of produce for good. And give a blessing on the surface of the earth.* And satisfy us from Your bounty, and bless this year like the good years. Blessed are You, God, who blesses the years.

10. Sound the shofar for our freedom, and raise a banner to gather in our exiles, and gather us together from the four corners of the earth. Blessed are You, God, who gathers in the scattered ones of His people, Israel.

11. Return our judges to us, as they were in the earliest times, and the ones who gave us counsel, as at first. And remove sorrow and groaning from us. And rule over us, You, God, all by Yourself, with loving-kindness and compassion. And we should come out righteous in judgement. Blessed are You, God, a King who loves righteousness and justice.

12. And for the slanderers let there be no hope, and may all evil be instantly destroyed. And all of Your enemies should be quickly cut off, and the rebellious sinners You should quickly uproot and smash and break and humble quickly in our day. Blessed are You, God, who breaks enemies and humbles rebellious sinners.**

13. On the righteous and on the devout and on the elders of Your nation and on the remnant of their scholars and on the righteous converts and on us, please bestow Your compassion, Lord our God, and give a good reward to all those who trust in Your name—in truth. And put our portion together with theirs, and we will not be embarrassed, because we have trusted in You. Blessed are You, God, Mainstay of and Assurer to the righteous.

14. And to Jerusalem, Your city, You should return with compassion and You should dwell there as You told us You would. And build it very soon and in our days, as an everlasting building. And may You speedily establish the throne of David within it. Blessed are You, God, who builds Jerusalem.

15. Make the offspring of David, Your servant, sprout forth quickly and raise his glory in Your salvation, because we hope for Your salvation all day. Blessed are You, God, who makes the glory of salvation flourish.

16. Hear our voice, Lord, our God, have pity and be compassionate to us, and accept our prayers with compassion and willingness, because You are a God who listens to prayer and supplication. And from before You, King, do not turn us away empty-handed, because You listen with compassion to the prayers of Your people. Blessed are You, God, who hears prayer.

17. Be pleased, Lord, our God, with your people, Israel, and with their prayers, and reinstate the service to the Holy of Holies in Your House, and sacrifices of Israel. And accept their prayers with love and willingness, and may the service of Your people, Israel, always be pleasing. And our eyes should see Your return to Zion with compassion. Blessed are You, God, who returns His divine Presence to Zion.

18. We thank You that You are the Lord, our God, and the God of our fathers, forever. You are the Rock of our lives, the Shield of our salvation, in every generation. We will thank You and tell Your praise for our lives which are given over into Your hand, and for our souls which are in safekeeping with You, and for Your miracles which are with us everyday, and for Your wonders and goodness that occur at all times— in evening, in the morning and in the afternoon. You are good, for You have not stopped Your compassion, and You are the Merciful One, for Your loving-kindness has not ceased.

19. Grant peace, goodness and blessing, graciousness, loving-kindness and compassion upon us and upon all Israel, Your nation. Bless us, our Father, together as one, with the light of Your face, because by the light of Your face, You have given us, Lord, our God, a Torah of life and a love of loving-kindness and righteousness and blessing and compassion and life and peace. It is good in Your eyes to bless Your peo-

ple, Israel, at all times and every hour with Your peace. Blessed are You, God, who blesses His people, Israel, with peace. May the words of my mouth and the meditation of my heart be acceptable to You, O Lord, my Strength and my Redeemer.

* In the winter replace this sentence with: "And bring dew and rain for a blessing."

** After the canonization of the Eighteen Benedictions, this particular paragraph was added; however, they are still referred to as the Eighteen Benedictions.

Source
"The Amidah," *The Chebar—Judeo/Christian Studies, News and You.* http://chebar0.tripod.com (accessed February 4, 2003).

ENDNOTES

Introduction

1. Jill Haak Adels, *The Wisdom of the Saints: An Anthology* (New York: Oxford University Press, 1987), p. 38.
2. Kenneth L. Woodward, "Talking to God," *Newsweek* (January 6, 1992), p. 38.

Chapter One

1. Jean LeClerc, Francois Vandenbroucke and Louis Bouyer, *A History of Christian Spirituality,* vol. 2, *The Spirituality of the Middle Ages* (New York: Seabury Press, 1982), p. 532.
2. Ibid.
3. Saint Teresa of Avila, *A Life of Prayer,* ed. James M. Houston (Portland, OR: Multnomah Press, 1983), p. 2.
4. Ruth A. Tucker and Walter Liefeld, *Daughters of the Church* (Grand Rapids, MI: Zondervan, 1987), p. 203.
5. Ibid.
6. Ian Adamson, *Bangor: The Light of the World* (Ireland: Bangor, 1979), p. 31.
7. Ibid., p. 32.
8. Ibid.
9. Ibid., p. 33.
10. Jesus' explanation indicated a definite paradigm breaker for the ascetic/monastic mind-set.
11. See our book *Welcoming a Visitation of the Holy Spirit* (Lake Mary, FL: Creation House, 1996), pp. 65-69, for an in-depth explanation of what happened to us and our church over this time of spiritual revival.

Chapter Two

1. Julian Stead, *Saint Benedict: A Rule for Beginners* (New York: New City Press, 1994), p. 105.
2. Mark Galli, "The Best There Ever Was," *Christian History* 64, vol. 28, no. 4 (1999), p. 10.
3. Dressler, et al., "St. Athanasius: The Life of St. Antony," *The Fathers of the Church: Early Christian Biographies,* trans. Sister Mary Emily Keenan (Washington, DC: The Catholic University of America Press, 1952), p. 137.

4. Ibid., pp. 142-145.

5. Philip Schaff, *History of the Christian Church*, vol. 3, *Apostolic Christianity* (Grand Rapids, MI: Eerdmans Publishing Co., 1910), p. 189.

6. Ibid.

7. Ibid.

8. William W. Simpson, *Jewish Prayer and Worship* (London: SCM Press Ltd., 1965), p. 13.

9. Rabbi Hayim Halevy Donin, *To Be a Jew* (New York: Basic Books, Inc., 1972), pp. 159-160.

10. Ibid.

11. Ibid., p. 159.

12. Ibid., p. 160.

13. Ibid., p. 161.

14. Simpson, *Jewish Prayer and Worship*, p. 28.

15. Ibid.

16. George Robinson, *Essential Judaism* (New York: Pocket Books, 2000), p. 180.

17. Helen Bacovicin, trans., *The Way of the Pilgrim* (New York: Image Books, 1978), p. 89.

18. Gordon MacDonald, *Ordering Your Private World* (Nashville, TN: Thomas Nelson, Inc., 1985), p. 29.

Chapter Three

1. Kevin Prosch, "Friend of God," copyright 1993 by 7th Time Music. All rights reserved. Used by permission.

2. Joachim Jeremias, *The Prayers of Jesus* (Philadelphia, PA: Fortress Press, 1978), p. 73.

3. Ibid., p. 68.

4. Ibid., p. 70.

5. *Strong's Greek-Hebrew Dictionary*, PC Study Bible ed., s.v. "sharath," "zakar," "yadah," "halal," "halel."

6. George Robinson, *Essential Judaism* (New York: Pocket Books, 2000), p. 53.

7. Jeremias, *The Prayers of Jesus*, p. 71.

8. Ibid., p. 75.

9. *Vine's Expository Dictionary of Biblical Words*, PC Study Bible ed., s.v. "continuing."

10. *Strong's Greek-Hebrew Dictionary*, PC Study Bible ed., s.v. "memorial."

11. Jeremias, *The Prayers of Jesus*, p. 78.

12. *The Apostolic Fathers* edited by Michael W. Holmes from materials translated by J. B. Lightfoot and J. R. Harmer, 2nd ed. (Grand Rapids, MI: Baker Book House, 1989), p. 146.

13. Ibid., p. 153.

14. Paul Bradshaw, *The Search for the Origins of Christian Worship* (New York: Oxford University Press, 1992), p. 190.

15. Ibid., p. 191.

16. Clifton Woltors, trans., *The Cloud of Unknowing and Other Works* (London: Penguin Books, 1961), p. 24.

17. Matthew Henry, PC Study Bible ed., commentary on "1 Cor. 15:32."

18. Rabbi Daniel Juster, personal e-mail to author, December 4, 2002.

19. Thomas Cahill, *How the Irish Saved Civilization* (New York: Doubleday Publishing Group, Inc., 1995), pp. 3-8.

20. Julian Stead, *Saint Benedict: A Rule for Beginners* (New York: New City Press, 1994), p. 112.

21. TV Turn-Off Week: Statistics About TV Habits. "Some Statistics on Television in America." SoundVision. http://www.soundvision.com/Info/misc/tvturnoff.asp (accessed November 27, 2002).

22. John Cassian, *Conferences,* trans. Colm Luibheid (New York: Paulist Press, 1985), p. 104.

23. Stead, *Saint Benedict: A Rule for Beginners,* p. 112.

Chapter Four

1. Sophy Burnham, *The Path of Prayer* (New York: Viking Compass, 2002), pp. 33-37.

2. Charles Colson, "BreakPoint with Charles Colson," (June 14, 2002), quoting Antonio Socci, *The New Persecuted.*

3. Rev. Johan Candelin, director of the WEA Commission for Religious Freedom, "Christian Persecution" (paper presented to the United Nations, Geneva, Switzerland, April 9, 2002).

4. *Allah—Teachings of Islam.* http://www.shirazi.org.uk/ (accessed October 2002).

5. Paul Fregosi, *Jihad in the West* (Amherst, New York: Prometheus Books, 1998), p. 17.

6. Osama bin Laden, interview by John Bell, *ABC News,* May 28, 1998.

7. See our book *Praying the Bible: The Book of Prayers* (Ventura, CA: Regal Books, 2002) for an explanation of how to do this.

8. Sam Anthony Morello, OCD, *Lectio Divina and the Practice of Teresian Prayer,* no. 158 (Washington, DC: Institute of Carmelite Studies, 1994), p. 11.

Chapter Five

1. Rabbi Daniel Juster, personal e-mail to author, December 4, 2002.
2. Campbell McAlpine, *The Practice of Biblical Meditation* (Glasgow, Scotland: HarperCollins Publishers, 1981), pp. 183-184.
3. Bishop Joseph Duffy, *St. Patrick Writes* (Dublin, Ireland: Messenger Publications, 1952), p. 12.
4. Lowrie J. Daly, *Benedictine Monasticism: Its Formation and Development Through the Twelfth Century* (New York: Sheed and Ward, 1965), p. 60.
5. Jean LeClerc, Francois Vandenbrouke and Louis Bouyer, *A History of Christian Spirituality,* vol. 2, *The Spirituality of the Middle Ages* (New York: Seabury Press, 1982), p. 44.
6. Sam Anthony Morello, OCD, *Lectio Divina and the Practice of Teresian Prayer,* no. 158 (Washington, DC: Institute of Carmelite Studies, 1994), pp. 7-8.
7. Ibid., p. 14.
8. Ibid., p. 22.
9. Ibid., pp. 20-21.
10. Martin Luther, *A Simple Way to Pray,* quoted in D. A. Carson, ed., *Teach Us to Pray* (Grand Rapids, MI: Baker Book House, 1990), p. 272.
11. Arnold Dallimore, *George Whitefield: The Life and Times of the Great Evangelist of the Eighteenth-Century Revival,* vol. 1 (London: Banner of Truth Trust, 1970), p. 80.
12. Ibid., pp. 80-83.
13. Ibid., p. 296.
14. Ibid., p. 251.

Chapter Six

1. John Cassian, *Conferences,* trans. Colm Luibheid (New York: Paulist Press, 1985), p. 139.
2. Rabbi Adin Steinsaltz, *A Guide to Jewish Prayer* (New York: Schocken Books, Israel Institute for Talmudic Publications, 2000), p. 34.
3. Ibid.
4. Ibid., p. 35.
5. *Strong's Greek-Hebrew Dictionary,* PC Study Bible ed., s.v. "hagah."
6. *The International Standard Bible Encyclopaedia,* PC Study Bible ed., s.v. "hagah," "higgayon."

7. Patrick D. Miller, *They Cried to the Lord: The Form and Theology of Biblical Prayer* (Minneapolis, MN: Fortress Press, 1994), p. 46.
8. Rabbi Daniel Juster, personal discussion with author, December 4, 2002.
9. Ibid.
10. Ibid.
11. Sam Anthony Morello, OCD, *Lectio Divina and the Practice of Teresian Prayer*, no. 158 (Washington, DC: Institute of Carmelite Studies, 1994), p. 9.
12. Jeanne Guyon, *Experiencing the Depths of Jesus Christ* (Sargent, GA: The Seed Sowers, 1975), n.p.
13. Ibid., pp. 7-8.
14. Morello, *Lectio Divina and the Practice of Teresian Prayer*, p. 13.
15. *Strong's Greek-Hebrew Dictionary*, PC Study Bible ed., s.v. "vain repetition."

Chapter Seven

1. Brother Lawrence, *The Practice of the Presence of God* (Springdale, PA: Whitaker House, 1982), p. 30.
2. R. M. French, trans., *The Way of a Pilgrim: A Classic of Orthodox Spirituality* (London: Triangle, 1930), pp. 8-18.
3. Ibid., p. 79.
4. Ibid., p. 80.
5. Ibid.
6. Ibid., p. 70.
7. Ibid.
8. Ibid., p. 60.
9. Ibid., p. 49.
10. Ibid., p. 50.
11. Ibid., p. 21.
12. Ibid., p. 93.
13. Thomas Dubay, *Fire Within* (San Francisco, CA: Ignatius Press, 1990), p. 76.
14. Saint Teresa of Avila, *The Collected Works of St. Teresa of Avila*, trans. Kieran Kavanaugh and Otilio Rodriguez, 3 vols. (Washington, DC: Institute of Carmelite Studies, 1976-1985), n.p.
15. Henri Nouwen, *The Way of the Heart: Desert Spirituality and Contemporary Ministry* (New York: HarperCollins Publishers, 1981), p. 49.
16. Dubay, *Fire Within*, pp. 69-70. Emphasis added.
17. Jeanne Guyon, *Experiencing the Depths of Jesus Christ* (Sargent, GA: The Seed Sowers, 1975), p. 80.

18. Ibid., pp. 86, 97.

19. Henri Nouwen, *The Way of the Heart: Desert Spirituality and Contemporary Ministry,* p. 34.

20. Ibid., p. 45.

21. Jean Daujat, *Prayer,* trans. Martin Murphy (New York: Hawthorn Books, 1964), p. 139.

22. Saint Francis, *The Little Flowers of St. Francis,* trans. E. M. Blaiklock and A. C. Keys (Ann Arbor, MI: Servant Books, 1985), pp. 2-3.

23. Source unknown.

24. Source unknown.

25. Dubay, *Fire Within,* p. 68.

26. Sam Anthony Morello, *The Ladder of Monks and Twelve Meditations* (Garden City, NY: Doubleday Image, 1978), p. 22.

SCRIPTURE INDEX

SUBJECT INDEX